Whispering Mind

Eternal Love story of Yin & Yang

Fable Poems on Life, Love & Joy of Living

Impressions

"Reflecting on and writing creatively about matters relating to the Consciousness will not only be refreshing, but also bring a sense of celebration to one's professional life."

- Sri Sri Ravi Shankar

"I found it educating on life, integrated approach on life, integrated approach of life management and its rejoicing. It's a wonderful effort of synthesizing such vast areas of yoga and spirituality in terms of poetry that is based on experiential knowledge."

- Swami Ramdev

"These poems cover all important aspects of life. Your compositions are most impressive and understandable by everyone. This book not only makes the people feel so happy while reading but also helps to develop the right framework of mind to take life in positive strides."

- Nara Chandrababu Naidu

"The Whispering Mind takes a sweepingly comprehensive view of life, both cosmic and real, and here and in all parts of the world and philosophises the actual life and actualises philosophy for those inclined to read philosophy into life and actualise it. I was particularly impressed by the poems "Outsourcing Love", "Chameleon Woman", "Taming the Monkey" to mention just three. These are real original thoughts flowing into poetic works. There is more intuition than just mere intellect driving the whole work. I am sure that this will cater to the growing needs of the modern mind in search of meaningful abstraction to escape from the painful finite life. Undoubtedly, a subtle spiritual dimension runs through the whole work as is natural in any Indian work on abstraction."

- S. Gurumurthy

"Profound and immensely readable, this is a collection that feeds the soul as well as the mind."

- The Week

"It's a unique compilation of true literary art and was great to read the creativity of your imagination."

- Mid Day Infomedia Ltd.

"The book will be an interesting read for fable poem lovers."

- 'Swagat' In flight magazine of Air India Limited

KHUSHWANT SINGH

49-E, SUJAN SINGH PARK
NEW DELHI - 110003

Dear Mr. Shashidharan

I read the first few poems, I was most impressed by your compositions and would be happy to see them in print.

Unfortunately there are few takers for poetry and publishers are reluctant to invest their money in books of poetry. Publishing & at our own cost is self defeating. As reviewers take no notice of these so you will have a job finding a good, honest publisher. I cannot help you find one.

I wish you the best of luck.

Yours
Khushwant Singh

Whispering Mind

Eternal Love story of Yin & Yang

Fable Poems on Life, Love & Joy of Living

K P Shashidharan

STERLING PUBLISHERS PRIVATE LIMITED

STERLING PUBLISHERS PRIVATE LIMITED
A-59, Okhla Industrial Area, Phase-II,
New Delhi-110020.
Tel: 26387070, 26386209; Fax: 91-11-26383788
E-mail: mail@sterlingpublishers.com
www.sterlingpublishers.com

Whispering Mind: *Eternal Love story of Yin & Yang*
© 2010, K P Shashidharan
ISBN 978 81 207 5263 4

All rights are reserved. No part of this publication may be reproduced, stored in a retrieval system or transmitted, in any form or by any means, mechanical, photocopying, recording or otherwise, without prior written permission of the original publisher.

Printed and Published by Sterling Publishers Pvt. Ltd., New Delhi-110 020.

भारत के नियंत्रक · महालेखापरीक्षक
COMPTROLLER & AUDITOR GENERAL OF INDIA

VINOD RAI

Foreword

I take pleasure in introducing the readers to 'Whispering Mind' written by Shri K.P. Shasidharan, an officer from the Indian Audit & Accounts Service. It was a pleasant revelation for me to know that an officer, dealing with numbers, debits, credits, Profit and Loss accounts and Balance Sheets could compose poetry interlinking significant aspects of life, love and spirituality.

Happiness is a state of mind. Quite often many of us do not even find time to relax and reflect. The poems in 'Whispering mind' take the reader through many existing twists and turns in life exposing a varied spectrum of life of human beings around the world.

Every poem in the book has different story to tell and a message to the reader to reflect on. The three themes in the book 'Spectrum of life', 'Rainbow of love' and 'Towards Awareness, Enlightenment and Bliss' are interconnected with an interesting and convincing story line on the drama called life that we enact in the world. The book has comprehensively dealt with wide variety of themes including poems on environmental issues, social themes like street children, street women, and other underprivileged sections of the society along with serious philosophical, existential, metaphysical and theological thoughts

I am particularly impressed by poems: 'Cleansing of the mind' 'Churning of the Mind lake', 'I am the Emperor', 'Living in Now.' And the 'Bliss'. These poems sensitize the reader towards accumulating pollution in the mind and heart and help churning the mind to make it strong, sublime and pure.

I am sure that the readers would be benefited by reading Shashi's 'Whispering Mind' as an enriching and enlivening experience.

(Vinod Rai)
Comptroller & Auditor General of India

Place: New Delhi
Date: April 23, 2010

*"In the end,
it's not going to matter
how many breaths you took,
but how many moments
took your breath away"*

-Shing Xion

Yin and Yang

WHISPERING MIND
IS DEDICATED TO MY YIN
AND YIN & YANG IN ME
YIN AND YANG IN YOU
AND EVERYONE WE LOVE!

ROMANCE OF WHISPERING MIND

Whispering Mind is a love story in poems. These poems are meant for all those who love life; like to live in love; believe in exploring and discovering the inner hidden energy in them; and linking it with the supreme energy vibes of the universe to optimise the joy of living.

There are poems on self help, travelogue, green poems, life stories, fables, social themes, life principles, fiction, mantra, tantra, mysticism, spirituality. The variety of subjects like shades of life, love and bliss encapsulating essential philosophy of life and ideas may appeal to every group of people: those who believe in celebrating joyful moments like Honeymoon, Valentine's Day, Father's Day, Mother's Day, Birthday, Marriage Anniversary and live in 'Now', the moment that ticks. Belief in the inner energy and its linkage with the supreme energy flow in the universe help those people who feel depressed, hungry for love or face tragedies in life. The mind can create catastrophic scenes. Misplaced anxieties, unwarranted worries take away the happiness. If we listen to and train the mind like a mind gymnast, negative feelings can be oriented towards healing the wounded soul and serving as lullaby for good sleep.

The poetry broadly falls into three themes bonded by the umbilical cord - the joy of living:

Theme One: Spectrum of Life

The poems are intended to take the reader for a virtual tour across continents, exposing to different life patterns. There are poems on philosophy and environment.

Message is simple: watching human behaviour, as a spectator may induce valuable lessons for good living.

Theme Two: Rainbow of Love

The poems express intense inner feelings experienced by the heart, mind and soul. These poems aim at taking the readers to the realms of man woman relationship, selfless feelings and emotions of falling in love, being loved; encompassing wide hues of love, pain, anguish, agony, anxiety, sorrow of separation, loneliness, insecurity and uncertainty of life.

Love gradually evolves through life's experiences bringing essential philosophy to enjoy living, genuine feelings, compassion and service to humanity; transcending to ultimate joy of falling in love with the Creator.

Theme Three: Journey to Awareness, Enlightenment and Bliss

This section starts with a green poem about visit to tree temple in Cambodia. The poems exhibit the existential riddle between destiny versus determinism taking to the beginning of the journey of life; and move towards taming the mind, cleansing of the mind, awareness, enlightenment and infinite bliss.

The book refers to life principles from Hinduism, Buddhism, Sufism, Christianity; curry-flavoured with Yoga, Pranayam, Meditation, Mantra, Tantra, Yantra. Some of these ideas, if practised in the right way, may help developing beautiful body, mind, and soul. These poems implicitly throw light on the four schools of thought - Raja Yoga, Karma Yoga, Bhakti Yoga and Gyana Yoga - explained in Bhagwad Gita, commented by Swami Vivekananda in his works.

A glimpse of theology and metaphysics is good for understanding the nuances of the river of life. Buddhist methodology of diagnosis, prognosis and prescription for elimination of suffering tenets of Jainism, Brahmanism, Sufism and Hinduism, flowering into Advaita philosophy of Adi

Shankaracharya are sprinkled in some of the poems. The spice of Vedas and Vedanta gives fresh aroma and delicacy for taking adversities in right stride.

The basic issues of mind and body gymnastics for bringing a beautiful mind in a beautiful body are explained in simple verses. The wisdom inherited by humanity from the treasure warehouses underlying some of the theological concepts like initiating the Kundalini[1] awakening - aligning the seven chakras[2] or energy circles of the spine - is comparable with scientific theories of self actualization.

Probabilities of winning the first race of life in search of the other half is nothing short of a marathon race of millions of the sperms to reach one or in selected cases two or three eggs to form life in the universe like Yang meeting Yin to form the whole from the parts! The first race of life, the journey of a soul, the Bird of Gold, the Bliss, Jai Ho My Web of Life, the Gift from God and many poems in the book narrate the story of determinism versus destiny, nature versus nurture, theism versus atheism, religion versus science, Yin versus Yang and diverse range of philosophical, existential, metaphysical, scientific thoughts.

The poems Wild Spider in the Sky, Zero and One Love Story, Jai Ho My Web of Life, Churning the Mind Lake, Dark Mother Goddess of Time, Cosmic Dance of Shiva and Shrichakra sing paeans of the energy linkage between the living and the universe, mythology and modern science. Ever expanding universe is perceived as the Cosmic Egg or 'Brahmandam'[3] with microcosm[4] called mind or 'Chidambaram'.

---

[1] In Indian yoga, a "corporeal energy" - an unconscious, instinctive or libidinal force or Shakti, envisioned either as a goddess or else as a sleeping serpent coiled at the base of the spine

[2] Seven major chakras or energy centres (also understood as wheels of light) are generally believed to exist, located within the subtle body

[3] The *Brahmanda Purana* is one of the eighteen *Mahapuranas*, a genre of eighteen Hindu religious texts and has been assigned the eighteenth place in almost all the lists of the *Puranas*

[4] a little world; especially : the human race or human nature seen as an epitome of the world or the universe

The romance of the Whispering Mind culminates gradually in the last few poems 'The Black Mother Goddess of Time', 'Cosmic Dance of Shiva', 'Churning of the Mind Lake', 'Shri Chakra' and 'The Bliss'.

Whispering Mind is thus a love story in verses of the energy vibes: Shakti and Shiva or Yin and Yang. Yin or Shakti is a metaphor for dynamic energy and Yang or Shiva[5], a metaphor for static form of cosmic energy. Some of the poems give further thoughts on worship of mother goddess, the cosmic womb, centrifugal and centripetal forces in the cosmic energy. All the poems conceived in the three themes are interconnected by the underlying central idea: optimising the joy of living, deriving maximum out of life by linking the inner strength with the external energy vibes.

Whispering Mind is my first book, though I had written some of these poems much earlier when I was living at Bath in UK. I had been a prolific freelancer with more than hundred 'middles' in editorial pages of leading national newspapers, I was also invited to talk to new writers at the instance of the then editor of The Hindustan Times on how to write 'middles'.

The format of Whispering Mind is the format in which thoughts took birth in my 'Chidambaram' – in the horizon of my mind as part of the cosmic dance of bliss. It matters little as long as readers rejoice!

---

[5] Shiva (meaning "Auspicious one"), is a major Hindu deity, and one aspect of *Trimurti* In the *Shaiva* tradition of Hinduism, Shiva is seen as the Supreme God

WHISPERINGS IN SEQUENCE

Foreword by Vinod Rai	5
Romance of Whispering Mind	7
The Eternal Love Story of Yin and Yang	15

THEME ONE:
Spectrum of Life: A Virtual Tour Across Continents

1.	Let us Visit our Mother's Exhibition	21
2.	Let us Visit Children's Exhibition	26
3.	Cultural Cocktail	38
4.	Fireballs in the Sky	43
5.	A Trekker's Story	47
6.	Tattooed Lovers	52
7.	Fury of the Wind	60
8.	Outsourcing Love	64
9.	Dangerous World	69
10.	Streets are our Home	73
11.	Chameleon Woman	79
12.	This Dance is our Life	84
13.	My Hubby Dear	88
14.	The Gymnast of the Mind	91
15.	Wild Spider in the Sky	95
16.	I Don't Remember	101
17.	Living Green with Nature	104
18.	I'm the Emperor	110

Theme Two:
Rainbow of Love

19.	Love Games on the Valentine Day	117
20.	Rainbow of Love	123
21.	The Religion of Love	127
22.	Energy Flow of Love	132
23.	Fragrance of Love	136
24.	Music of Love	140
25.	God in the Holy Cave	144
26.	Nest Becomes a Cage	150
27.	The Gift From God	155
28.	The Zero and One Love Story	161
29.	It Rained in my Mind	172
30.	Story of Love and Envy	176
31.	Lost Lullaby	180
32.	Sand Dunes of Time	184
33.	Twilight not Merging into Night	189
34.	You be your Mom you be your Baby	192
35.	Living in Now	196
36.	Jai Ho My Web of Life	199

Theme Three:
Towards Awareness, Enlightenment, and Bliss

37.	Green Poem: Trees in Temple	207
38.	Queuing for 'Darshan'	211
39.	Whispering Mind	215
40.	The First Race of Life	221
41.	The Bird of Gold	225
42.	Journey of a Soul	232
43.	River of Life	235
44.	Eternal Energy Flow	241
45.	You Gifted the Sun its Energy	246
46.	Taming the Monkey	249
47.	Cleansing of the Mind	255
48.	Maya called Life	259
49.	The Awakening	267
50.	Churning the Mind Lake	272
51.	The Black Mother Goddess of Time	280
52.	Cosmic Dance of Shiva	286
53.	Shri Chakra: Geometry of the Seed of Creation	298
54.	The Bliss	315

LIST OF WONDERS AND OTHER PLACES CITED IN WHISPERING MIND

1. Niagara Falls – Maid of the Mist 57
2. Grand Canyon and Colorado River 31
3. Mount Rushmore – The Four Presidents 22
4. The Last Remaining Ancient Wonder of the World and the New Seven Wonders 27, 32-35, 37
5. Los Angeles, Hollywood, California, US 27
6. Las Vegas, Nevada, US 29
7. Interlaken, Switzerland 47
8. Giza Pyramid Complex, Cairo, Egypt 35
9. Taj Mahal in Moonlight, Agra, India 27
10. Christ the Redeemer: Rio de Janeiro, Brazil 32
11. Chichen Itza: Yucatan, Mexico 32
12. Machu Picchu: Cuzco, Peru 33
13. Colosseum: Rome, Italy 29
14. Great Wall of China: Beijing, China 58
15. Petra: Jordan 35
16. Burj Khalifa, Dubai 37
17. New York: Night Club, Statue of Liberty 38
18. Burning Twin Towers, Ground Zero: Manhattan, New York 44
19. Paris, France 31
20. Avon River, Abbey, Bath, UK 61
21. Vithiri, Wayanad, Kerala, India 104
22. Shravanabelagola, Karnataka, India 91
23. Amarnath Yatra: Ice Shivalinga, Srinagar, India 144
24. Sam Sand Dunes, Jaisalmer, Rajasthan, India 184
25. Kuwait City, Kuwait. 192
26. Silicon Valley, San Francisco, US 199
27. Ta Prohm Temple, Angkor Wat, Cambodia 207
28. Bodhgaya Temple, Bodhgaya, Bihar, India 215
29. Confluence of Indus River and Zanskar River at Nimu, Ladakh, India 235
30. Manasa Sarovar and Mount Kailash: Tibetan Himalayas, Tibet 272
31. Chidambaram Temple, Tamil Nadu, India 293
32. Shringeri, Karnataka, India 298

The Eternal Love Story of Yin and Yang

The eternal love story of Yin and Yang is based on the energy equation of Einstein; E=MC Squared, where E is energy and M is mass and C is speed of light. The energy equation establishes that energy and mass are different manifestations of the same thing and cannot be destroyed, and if mass can be converted into energy it will yield tremendous quantity of energy. Mass and energy can appear and disappear in various forms and the sum total of energy and mass remains the same in the universe over the ages as proved by the theory of Relativity.

At higher realms of science and religion, physics and metaphysics, explanations to the origin of universe and life in the universe converge. The age of the universe calculated as per Hindu mythology and that of quantum mechanics and particle physics gives more or less the same conclusions and results. In a sense, Energy and Mass are complementary parts of one whole, like Yin and Yang complementing many phenomena in the macrocosm and microcosm. In Whispering Mind, science, religion, physics, metaphysics, facts of life, fiction, story, legend and fantasy are intermixed to weave the romantic story of Yin and Yang as incarnated in Babe and Darling.

All mighty Almighty is the great Maker of his famous brand live human robots amongst various other products and things in the universe for which He is well known! The Maker manufactures, among other things, human toy robots with twin ventilators-invisible Mind Machine and ticking time machine called heart, programmed with a certain number of pre determined ticks, hung in the cavern of the chest wrapped in the rib cage right at the centre. The Maker also inserts a chip in the head of the human robot as brain with very less capacity than the Maker. The Maker is careful that his toy robot should not in any eventuality be transformed into a Frankenstein Monster, capable of challenging Him.

Though the human robot has a brain chip of less IQ, he thinks he knows too much and has the audacity, aggressive characteristics and arrogance to disrespect and challenge his Maker in various ways with his limited perspective and understanding of complex hidden mysteries of nature. Having been endowed with lesser brain power than his Creator, human robot takes considerable time to understand a little bit of the mysteries and secrets of the world and he thinks he knows too much. In fact the extent of the totality of knowledge in the universe which is to be unravelled, the extent of knowledge so far unravelled and to what extent human beings know form part of conjecture of the unknown.

As per mythology there was abyss or Yin in the very beginning and light or Yang came subsequently. They have been living together in the Cosmic Womb. They are present everywhere in the universe as complementary parts making a whole, like polarity of the magnet, or negative and positive energy flows of the electricity, day and night, light and darkness. From the eternal energy pool, as per belief, except the souls who have not attained Nirvana or extricated themselves from the Cycles of life and death and rebirth or the Wheel of Life, circumambulate the universe seeking opportunities for life.

In Whispering Mind, Yin appears in the form of Babe and Yang appears in the form of Darling. They come from the eternal energy pool or the REAL WORLD and play the Drama called Life in the UNREAL world that appears to be real in the illusion called Maya. Yin and Yang have been present in every living being as part of life.

Babe and Darling, being part of the energy vibes of the universe and having been endowed with Mind Machine, circumambulate in the speed of mind waves in mind times to oversee what is happening in the world. Their rivers of life meander through varied life experiences narrated in the book, urging to reach the destination in the Ocean of Consciousness to join as waves, to be evaporated to form clouds and to pour down as rain to be born as a stream in the womb of glacier somewhere in the mountains.

This is identical with the Drama called Life of the soul in the Cycles of life, death and rebirth or the Wheel of Life. Here the journey starts from the sum total of the energy pool of the universe, participating in the first race of life and completing all the scenes in the drama till the final tick of the time machine hung at the heart is done as in bliss for merging into the energy pool or the Ocean of Supreme Consciousness of the universe.

In order to enjoy and appreciate the eternal love story of the eternal lovers Yin and Yang, it is recommended to read the book as a fable from the beginning including the introductory explanations and poems in sequence as presented in the book.

Theme One
SPECTRUM OF LIFE: A VIRTUAL TOUR ACROSS CONTINENTS

Amazing shades emerge when life passes through the prism of experience. Life is short to have all experiences. Being a spectator helps. Many leaves can be taken into our own lives without undergoing the turmoil of certain experiences!

In this section the reader is taken to a virtual tour to nature's and man-made wonders, life styles and responses of human beings in different parts of the Planet Earth to get the aroma and taste of pulsating life.

The connecting central theme in these poems is a being, an onlooker enjoying and learning from life patterns and responses of people of different socio-cultural milieu for making a difference, sharing happiness and values that make life worth living and handing over a better world to the future generations.

Poem-1

LET US VISIT OUR MOTHER'S EXHIBITION

We meet Yin and Yang as Babe and Darling in this poem. The story begins when they go for honeymoon and decide to see their mother's exhibition.

[Here in Whispering Mind, Babe and Darling represent the primordial female and male energy existing since the very beginning, which cannot be contained in time, space or geographical domains. They travel all over the Cosmos since the very beginning in the speed of mind waves, faster than light or electromagnetic waves, any media known to science, encircling the universe in mind times!]

During the exhibition the couple comes to know that their mother is critically ill. They want to help their mother!

I

Babe, don't you remember
Our honeymoon voyage
We were at Niagara
On the **'Maid of the Mist'**
We felt scared when the fall
Thundered in the heart

You clinched me tight in fright
Close to my chest
The milky whirlpool of the fall
Shook the vessel in rage

Beholding the beauty
Of the rainbow in your eyes
Looking deep into me
Intoxicated with the elixir of life
You told:
"We should miss not
The greatest exhibition
Of our Mother Nature!"

You whispered: "Darling,
Money may come
And money may go
And we too will go
It's once in a lifetime experience
Let us see more
Of the Mother's exhibition!

She exhibits
At Mount Rushmore
Yellow stone
Bryce, Zion, Grand
Banff galleries
And elsewhere!"

2

You convinced me
Our Mother continues
Sculpturing for millions of years
Tirelessly improving
The best of her paintings
Sculptures, architectures to perfection!

She works on deep black hills
Granite, marble, sandstone
Creating towers, waterfalls, geyser basins
Sculpturing pink cliffs
Wind carved arches and painted deserts
Crimson 'butt's, crazy horse
Adam and Eve!

3

Good we could opt for
The helicopter ride
We flew through the walls
Painted in flames
The largest exhibition halls
Amidst breathtaking views
Ever-changing hues
Of the blooming stones!

You went in panic
The helicopter plunged
Down the ravines
Five thousand feet
Abysmal depths

Towards
The Scorpion Creek;
Where once planes collided
Ending lives of tourists in inferno!

We witnessed a tourist
Diving into the ecstasy
From the edge
Terminating his journey
Falling into the green blue
Rapids of the Colorado River!

The artist was indifferent
Stopped not
Carving the mountains
Recreating rock walls
Tables of the Sun towers
Gorgeous holes, arches, bridges
Giving dimensions incredible
To architectural wonders
Polishing and painting
In blood red and fire tinge!

4

Incredible
We were invited to the Summit
On the Mount at Mount Rushmore
With the four great US presidents
Washington, Jefferson, Lincoln, and Roosevelt

Made the impossible possible
They travelled in time
To help curing the Mother
Of the rising fever-
A culmination of our follies!

Diagnosed the illness
How she got infected
From her greedy children
Made
Her ugly, pale and sick
How her children
Should work to save her:

"Children, give mother
Fresh air, water, food
Never ever keep
Her under stress
Never make her inhale
Injurious toxic fumes
Never ever make her
Drink contaminated
Toxic, waste water!

Let her land, mountains, forests
Oceans, lakes, rivers be clean
Let her animals, birds, pets
Organisms, microorganisms
Live in harmony!

Allow her reconvert
Her polluted home clean
For her children
Grandchildren
And great grandchildren!"

Poem-2
LET US VISIT CHILDREN'S EXHIBITION

After mother's exhibition, Babe wants Darling to take her to the children's exhibition.
After witnessing a few, she desires to have a sky home in the vertical city.

I
"Money may come
And money may go
We too will go
It is once in a lifetime
Let us visit the children's exhibition too";
Babe, you whispered
After enjoying
A few galleries of our Mother!

The children made great wonders
Stupendous all over the world
But not so enduring in comparison
With those of the great Mother!

Hundreds of manmade wonders
Ancient, medieval and modern
What to see and what not to see
Where to begin and when to begin!

We began
Before the icon of love
The **Taj Mahal** was bathing in moonlight
She smiled
Suspending our dream in the horizon
Bringing music, songs
Rhythm and dance
Enlivening our six senses
In the splendour of love!

2

We were there in Hollywood
At Universal Studios
The entertainment capital of LA!

Roaming the theme parks
Shoulder to shoulder
Marx Brothers, Marilyn Monroe
Lucille Ball, Woody Woodpecker
Andy Panda, the Flintstones
Scooby-Doo and Shaggy
Dracula, Frankenstein
The Wolf Man!

We were amidst the clowns
Exploring tons and tons of thrills
Fun, adventure, comic and laughter!

We rode through the 'Jurassic Park'
Splashing through waters
Escaping roaring man eating dinosaurs
Vicious raptors, venomous spitters!

We faced the horrifying
The 'Revenge of the Mummy'
Experiencing the limits
Of 'Fear Factor'
Meeting Dracula in his fortress
The house of the horrors!

It was fun to ride with the Simpsons
Laughing at the Krustyland!
Joining 'Terminator 2-3D'
In a cyber war of the robots!

We had to jump out of the seat
In water, mist, and wind
In the fairyland
With Shrek and Donkey
At 'Shrek 4D' rides!

Spellbound were we
Seeing Steven Spielberg's
"War of the Worlds"!

Special effects made
The 'Backdraft' show virtual!
Fireballs, heat, explosions
Inferno was raging in the warehouse
In the rain of red hot ashes
Inferno swallowed the theatre!

3

'Babe, if you don't mind
Let us fly now to Las Vegas
The Entertainment Capital of the World
Let us be sleepless at Vegas
In the city that never sleeps!
Let us see the ultimate shows
In the Sin City of the World!"!

Let us go for 'Love' at the 'Mirage'
Let us pay tribute to the Beatles!
Let us listen to Cher and Elton John
At the Colosseum at Caesars Palace!
Let us join singing with Celine Dion
'I'm alive' at the Caesars' Palace!

Let us meet the Lion King in Vegas
The last wild place on earth!
Let us dress up and show up
'Tony n' Tina's Wedding'!

Let us watch the 'Tournament of Kings'
The greatest magic show at the Greek Isles
Let us be at the magic show at Monte Carlo
We saw Phantom at the Venetian
Hysterically funny Blue Man Group!

Let us be at Chippendales at the Rio
Enjoying the Ultimate Girl's Night Out!
Let us be in 'Midnight Fantasy' at Luxor!

Let us see girls getting real wet
Before us at the Treasure Island!

Let us be there at' Zumanity'
Let us see the pussy cat dolls
At the Flamingo Hotel at the Strip!
The show girls and Crazy Girls must go on
Come Paris in La Femme!
Let us get titillated at the Peepshow
With Holly Madison in the Strip!

Let us see how 'Marriage Can Be Murder'
At the Four Queens!
Let us listen to 'Menopause'
The musical at Hilton!
Let us be there
V the Ultimate Variety Show
In the 'Miracle Mile Shops'
At the Planet Hollywood!

    4

Babe, we had Champagne toast
Before the helicopter flight over Vegas
We flew over Glitter Gulch
The golden towers of Mandalay Bay
Soaring past the dancing waters
Cruising over the Bellagio and
The towering New York New York Hotel!
Incredible show world

The Las Vegas Strip
Immersed fully in millions of neon lights!
We flew seeing down
The Luxor' searching laser beams!
The Freemont Street Experience
The Stratosphere tower!
The Eiffel Tower at Paris in Vegas!

5

Before leaving Vegas
We soared like birds
In another helicopter ride
Over Las Vegas, Boulder City
Over Hoover Dam
And Lake Mead
The largest manmade lake in the US!

We landed at the Colorado River
Enjoyed the Hualapai Tribal Land
Tasted the tasty Champagne
And boarded for the pontoon boat ride!

We rafted right through
The white water rapids
With Hualapai Indian guide
Down the Colorado River
Seeing the hidden bowels
Of the Grand Canyon Basin
Colourful virgin rocky cliffs, waterfalls!
Then came the scenic rim bus tour

To Eagle Point to be ready
For the Grand Canyon Sky Walk!
Holding hands we walked over
The suspended Glass Bridge
Beyond the canyon walls
Seeing four thousand feet down
The Colorado River flowing!

6

We flew in January
To the "River of January"
To Rio de Janeiro!

Jesus stood tall atop on the hunch
On the Corcovado mountain
In the Tijuka forest park alone!
In the cloudy misty morning
Arms opened
Heart filled with love!

He looked at the mountain ranges
Below the city, the sea and beyond
Gave us forever a permanent hug
And blessed us
The **Christ the Redeemer**!

7

Babe
Do you remember, still
When we flapped our wings to Mexico
In the mouth of the well of **Chichen Itza**

Welcomed us
The "Witches of Water"
The 'Maya' temple of Kukulkan
The El Castillo castle!

It was the spring equinox
In the light and shadow effect
We saw
The plumed serpent God
Crawling
On the Temple of Kukulkan!

8

When we landed In Peru
Followed the Inca trail
The mysterious
Machu Picchu
Stood nestled on a small hilltop
Above the Urubamba Valley!

Babe you loved
The "Lost Cities"
From the Funerary Rock Hut
Viewing the seamless
Elegant green paradise!

9

Good we arrived
In Rome on a Good Friday
Joined the Pope
Who led torch lit procession -

'Way of the Cross'
Near the Roman **Colosseum**
Built by the emperor Titus

My love
Do you remember now
While encircling
The elliptical amphitheatre
We pretended
The Roman regal couple
Viewing gladiatorial fights, chariot races
Mock batties, wild beast chases

You felt sorry for those
Wild animals and people
Massacred in cold blood in games!

10

Amazing were the endless waist chains
Gifted to most of the mountains
In China by her great kings
The spirit of the **Great Wall** !
Those kings had built
Fortifications all over
Stretching all along the north
Started by Qin Shi Huangdi
In two thousand years ago
Twenty dynasties thereafter!
Climbing up on the wall
The symbol of defence against war

Peace against aggression
We knew how they defended
Against the invading Huns
The nomadic tribes from the north

11

Babe, you liked the cruising
Memorable excursion along the Nile
Alexandria port to Cairo;
Seeing the royal necropolis –
The great pyramids of Giza,
The great sphinx and the Valley temple!

The slanting slopes of the pyramids
Captured the slanting rays of the Sun
Helped the souls of the Pharaohs
And their concubines
Climbing up towards
The sky to join Gods in the heaven!

12

In the desert land of Jordan
We wondered seeing **Petra**
The rock carved rose red city
In full of mysterious charm!
On the slope of Mount Hor
Hidden in the rugged mountains
The place in the desert was designed
By God for the Jewish People!

We were told the woman was gifted
With the two wings of a great eagle
She might fly to Petra
The place prepared for her
In the desert;
When Jerusalem falls
Before the Antichrist
In "Prophesy:
The Second coming of Jesus Christ"!

13

On the way back
Flying away from Jordan
Babe, I remember
You desired to be inside
The mightiest phallus
 Ever erected by any man
On the planet earth
Penetrating half a mile
Into the womb of the sky
Exhibiting bulging bundled tubes around!

You showed me the manmade
Palm Jumeirah island in the haze
Long stretches of the distant desert landscape
Merging into the azure Persian Gulf
From the observatory!
You whispered:
"My Darling!
Let us have a sky home

In the vertical city
This longest wily in the world-**Burj Khalifa**;
That beats Taipei 101
Thousand feet down below majestically!"

The tallest structure stood
Known for beautiful rendition to artistry
Engineering genius
An overriding hallucination
Vision, ecstasy, dream suspended
Never before in the horizon
Since the Stone Age man
Came out of his cave!

Poem-3

CULTURAL COCKTAIL

The couple visits one of the night clubs in New York.

[Yin & Yang have been very familiar watching the human beings since the days of Adam and Eve roaming naked; not even realizing that they were naked like animals, till they ate the forbidden fruit from the Tree of Knowledge under the influence of the serpent in the Garden of Eden!]

The human animal had since moved from his cave home to skyscrapers wandering over millions of years learning, relearning, doing and redoing, adopting and adapting varied life styles, endeavouring to make difference in living, loving and enjoying life.

Babe and Darling leave no chance to observe and learn from experience. They notice some valuable principles of life there.

In the ancient land of tribes
Of Algonquian and Iroquois[1]
Where tribes and buffaloes
Multiplied their breed
Once uninterrupted!

In front of the Statue of Liberty –
The statue which illuminates the world

---

[1] a member of any tribe

Cultural Cocktail

I told Babe:
"It's a gene mix
Of White, Black, Brown, Yellow, Hispanic-
In this Melting Pot called New York!"

Her eyes were lost in the race
Of skyscrapers' conquest of the sky
In the gargantuan forest
Of glass, steel and concrete
I saw in her eyes then neon lights
In millions, flickering like stars!

While strolling along
The Brooklyn Bridge
Letting eyes to swim over the waves
In the East river
We saw the cultural cocktail around
Begetting futuristic citizens of the world!

Broadway was inundated by the neon lights
The great white way was transformed
Into a glittering canyon
We went to a night club in the Big Apple
To join folks who boozed and rocked in rhythm!

The human animals were in ecstasy
In psychedelic pulsating lights
Tonsured, waxed, tattooed, dyed
Heads, bodies and organs in style !

Pierced ears, noses, lips, eyebrows, tongues
Breasts, navels, genitals and where not
She-men, He-women, Lady-men, Boy-girl
Made life alien, kicking, glitzy and out of the world!

Pony tails, hair dyed in multi hues
Green, yellow, blue, violet, red, pink
Bizarre styles: some styled like
Conical, cactus like thorny bushes and grass
Glued to stand like pyramids on the head !

Guys, gays, lesbians, transvestites
Sadists-masochists and trendsetters
Rocked hard, bringing new lyrics, melody
Music, rhyme, rhythm and colour!

I saw red lips of a blonde
Blossoming like a lotus flower
To lock in hers fat smoked black lips
Of her African boyfriend!
When released
Black lips whispered
Into her diamond adorned ears
I overheard dancing nearby:
"Won't you give me a baby?"'
"Sure" she joked, "If you can predict
The colour of our baby!"

I murmured to Babe:
"See, colour is no bar
Man loves woman!"

Jazz music flowed in dim light
Drunken men and women swam
Like fish in Music Lake

A cute Chinese girl danced well
With her tall Yankee boyfriend

Babe whispered:
"Human beings
Are one and the same
Race no bar, colour no bar
Language no bar
Woman loves man!"

When long-legged two youths
Swayed like trees in the music storm
Their long hair danced behind
Bewildered I looked at Babe:
"Bet, gay couple or lesbians?"

When they engaged in hugging
She muttered:
"I don't know their sex
How does it matter?
Anyway, world is great
 When man and woman are crazy in love
Man loves woman
Man loves man too!
Woman loves man
Woman loves woman too!

Race: No matter
Religion: No issue
Region: No problem
Colour: No bar

Money: Not a worry
Gender: Makes no difference
No taboo for sex or love
What matters is love
The opium of the body
Mind and soul" !

Poem-4

FIREBALLS IN THE SKY

The couple visits Manhattan again.

Haunting memories of one of the worst tragedies in human history- September 11, 2001 in New York disturb them, bringing nightmares into reality.

They notice that human mind can be so destructive, a raging inferno, and that we need to save the humanity first from the catastrophe continuously being created by evil minds and instill love, affection, compassion and concern!

The couple wonders: Can we hand over the world we inherited to our grandchildren as a world of love, care and joy!

Fireballs in the sky
Fiery explosions
Raging inferno
Amidst engulfing hungry raging flames
Dark clouds of smoke, fumes and dust
Jumped out
Human beings with debris!

Not a dream
Not a horror film
The real horrific
Massacre in the sky !

The Twin Brothers collapsed
The epitome of human genius
Melted into ashes and rubbles
Cremating human beings alive!

Mind indoctrinated
Head brainwashed
Men incarnated as devils
Continued poisoning minds
With hatred, anger, enmity
Envy, violence, destruction
Piloted the aircrafts right into
The heart of the Twin Brothers
Bombed the conscience of the humanity!

First time I was at the observatory
At the Twin Towers in Manhattan
The symbol of civilization
On the Planet Earth
With my friend
Who worked at the Towers
With his family !

Overwhelmed with excitement
Amazed by the pulsating world down
I felt I was at the top of the world
Breathing down the skyline
I screamed in joy
While the towers
Swayed in wind!

Witnessing the Ground Zero now
The graveyard of my friend
And many thousands like him
I stood in prayer
With his wife and baby
Tears rolled out of my eyes
For all the lives cremated alive!

Amidst the horrendous terror
Living with horrific memories
Of those who lost lives and wounded!
Amidst those devils who are dogged
To kill the innocents out of the blue
Will the shocked humanity
Be ever the same?

My heart ached with pain:
How do we put off the raging blaze
Of terrorism in the minds !
Can we get on the roots
Of anger, hostility, vengeance
Human beings hating human
Human beings becoming inhuman ?

Can we instill in the minds
Love and kindness
Can we kindle the mind
With sparks of compassion and care ?

Can we leave the Planet Earth
For our children
Grandchildren
A world of love, care and joy?

Poem-5

A TREKKER'S STORY

The couple meets a trekker at Interlaken in Switzerland during one of the trekking expeditions on the Alps. They invite him for a drink and hear his story.
The experienced trekker had been clambering different difficult mountain peaks! And this is his life story.

Do you remember, Babe
The trekker we met
At Interlaken
In the heart of the Swiss Alps
Between the twin lakes
Thunersee and Brienzersee
In the hikers' paradise!

The backpacker adventurer
We interacted while
Interlaken walking
Spent his life
Skydiving, paragliding
Canyoning, bungee jumping
Ice-climbing, glacier hiking
Biking, rafting, skating
Hang-gliding, skiing and trekking!

Heavy rucksack
Pulled down his shoulders
Ankles ached
Muscles strained
Sore feet pained in boots
But balanced his body
On the glacier path!

He was on a mission
Climbing up virgin peaks
After hiking many a marked trails
In the Jungfrau region!

Weren't we then
Upon the Jungfraujoch
After the rollercoaster journey
At the highest railway station in Europe?

It was indeed nice to invite him for a drink
At Schilthorn-Piz Gloria-
The first revolving restaurant
In the world?

Hey, we were listening to him
His adventure filled life
While wining
Seeing spectacular three sixty degree
Panorama of glittering snow-capped peaks!

A Trekker's Story

Great trekker was he
Conquered some of those peaks
Climbing with his co-trekker
Whom he loved from the core of his heart!

He told eyes filled in tears
He had met her on the way
She had joyfully shared
His sleeping bag one night
And thereafter every night!

And after the mission
Decided them to trek together
Sharing the body warmth
In the chilled atmosphere
And scaling steadily
The mountain called life!

He confessed pointing out
Some snow-capped Alps' peaks
That he was indeed clambering
The toughest of all peaks
Of all the treks he ever had!

Wasn't it more risky
More dangerous and slippery;
Than all those glacier heights
He could conquer with ease!

Narrow were the gorges
Riskier were the sharp cruel razor edges
Body and mind got bruised badly
But he loved the trek more as he loved her
Wasn't he ready to give her his life?

One day she confessed to him
She co-trekked with other climbers too
As sharing life path thrilled her always
Somewhere while co-trekking with someone
Sharing sleeping bag in some night
She didn't know she was gifted with something
That grew in her making her exhausted
That she passed on to co-trekkers thereafter!

He knew she was generous to give it to him too
He lost interest in all trekking
There was no stamina, urge left in him
Abandoned in life trek by his co-trekker
He noticed a stranger in one morning
Staring at him in agony in the mirror!

He could see deep canyons, ravines,
Weathered barren Rockies all on his face!
He saw his expanding desert like forehead
Receding towards the crown of his head!
Remained only a few greying patches
Like oases in a hostile alien desert land!

A Trekker's Story

Sagging double chin
Juxtaposed bizarrely
Like a second face
Above the neck staring!

Teeth were long
Dark yellow and sparse
Most of them chewed up
Almost by germs
Blurred was his fading eyesight though
He could see his crumbling physique
Weathered like a dried apricot!

He realized
He was at the peak all alone
Getting a co-trekker wasn't easy so often!

The left patch of dried grass
On his desert sort of head
Swayed in the cool breeze
Of a wintry morning
Like a flag hoisted
On the top
Of the mountain peak!

Poem-6

TATTOOED LOVERS

The couple meet Boo and Julia in Paris, the beautiful romantic city known for love and passion. Boo and Julia live on the top of their Studio accommodation there. The couple gets fascinated by their experiments with life, love and bliss in a totally innovative style to keep love alive and kicking.

I

Hey Babe
How can we forget?
Those paradise days
In the city of Paris!

Seine river cruising
Eiffel Tower dinner
Shows after shows!

Le Moulin Rouge
Le Crazy Horse
Le Crazy Girls
Le Femme
Le Lido de Paris
Le Paradis Latin
The great Parisian shows!

We were happy
L 'Open Hope-on
Hop-off Tour
The Louvre Museum
Mona Lisa
The 'Arc de Triomphe'
Avenue des Champs-Elysees!

Place de la Concorde
Sacre Coeur Basilica
Notre Dame Cathedral
Centre Georges Pompidou!

Going to La Defense
Versailles
Having Champagne
At Champagne!

Hi Babe
How can we forget Paris?
The tattoo lovers we knew
They lived and danced
Above the studio
Where we lived!

2

"I love you, my skin-head
You're wonderful
You excite me to infinity
With crazy tattoos on you";

Amazed she looked
At his tattooed physique
Held him close to her bosom!

"Don't you appreciate
What does my body speak?":
Queried Boo
Looking in her eyes!
Stroking his tonsured head
She cooed like a bird;

"Marvellous are these patterns
But Boo! Didn't you have a pony tail
When I saw you first in a pub?"

"Damn! Do I care pony tail?
Fed up with old fashioned fun!
Guess meaning
Of iconography on my head?"

"Hey! God! Isn't a monster?
Tell me, what's this cloud sort of stuff?
Terrific! Incomprehensible!
Classic! Great! Obscure! Cute"!

"Don't you worry, sweetheart
It's beyond my dull head too
Artist told me
It's his magnum opus
The Crazy Mind-the-Devil"

Tattooed Lovers

"You're the type of man
Who sustain my interest lifelong!
You've everything that I search
Pyramids! Volcanoes!
Spaceships! Spikes!
Dragons! Eagles! Scorpions!

Flora, fauna, geometrical designs
And geographical wonders!
A painter's delight!
An art lover's passion!

There remains a worry for me
Life is too short Boo
For enjoying these amazing tattoos
On your massive muscular macho
Male Body canvass!"

"Julia, my love
It's my ambition
Be the Tattoo-King
The most tattooed man
Walking on the Planet Earth!

Till a little skin is left
I'll get my body tattooed
With complex iconography-
The best artistic creation
Ever drawn
On human body canvass!"

3

Boo laid down naked
Feeling great
Exhibiting his tattoos
Breathing in and out!

He expanded his chest
Rolling on the bed
Crawling and bending
Boasting the hidden meanings
Of the patterns!
And why and how
He loved them
Sticking on him forever!

Julia went crazy
Hugging and kissing him
Stroking, biting him and his tattoos!
Stepping on his chest

Mounting in ecstasy
Julia pinched his cheeks
Slapped him in joke and posed:
"Boo
When you'll become
The King of Tattoos
Won't you like me
The Queen of Tattoos?"

"That's great
 I like that, Darling!
But how can you
Be the Queen of Tattoos
With no tattoos at all?

Isn't it too unexciting?
No tattoos:
On your lovely paper white live skin
Having no masterpieces?
Enchant me, seduce me, Julia
Enthral me, hypnotise me, mesmerize
Entrance me, with titillating tatoos?

Julia, my baby
 You've gotten
Fabulous body
Voluptuous, amazing curves !

Gorgeous mounts
Sexy cleavages
Any tattoo artist will go crazy
Working on the sexy canvass
Creating a magical charming world
Of incredible Tattoo Land on you!

I want to make you
More breathtaking
Than canyons land
More overwhelming
Than Niagara Falls

More mysterious
Than Pyramids of Egypt!
I want my babe that way
More inspiring
Than Great Wall of China!
More wonderful
Than Eiffel Tower!
Or St. Louis Arch!
More beautiful
Than the Taj Mahal!"!

"Boo! You're my He man
Let me have a lovely Picasso
On the silky curves of my tummy!
A cutie Van Gogh on my thighs!
A crazy Gauguin on my bottom!
A grand Dali on my groin!
Umm! I remember now
I love a Husain's
Galloping Horse on my Bum!"

"Don't you worry, my queen
You're going to have what you love
Astounding wonders
Awe inspiring, love inciting
Romantic artistic marvels
All over your body;
Tattooed, making you
A walking fabulous gallery
A tattoo merry wonderland on move!

I won't allow, I promise
The canvass will go no waste
Damn! We've got to be
The most tattooed lovers
On the Planet Earth
Must be documented so
By the Guinness Book of Records!"

    4

Boo and Julia went crazy
Spent months in admiring
Worshipping each other and their tattoos
 Finally got fed up with them
 And their never changing tattooed skins!

Life bickering began
Boredom sets in abundance
Exhibitions increased manifold
Admirers multiplied a galore!

Life rolled by
Increased open, inclusive
And exclusive, exhibitions!
Tattoo exhibitions to admirers
New life, new lovers, novel styles
Creative, exploring, unravelling!

When fidelity and loyalty
Are lost in relationship
Can mere iconography of tattoos
Hold lovers together in life?

Poem-7

FURY OF THE WIND

After touring Europe, England, Wales and Ireland, the couple stayed at Bath for few days. While living at Bath, the picture post card perfect town in UK, known for Roman Baths, the couple meets a saxophonist at the city centre. This is his life story.

The couple realises that life doesn't give too many opportunities. What makes life beautiful is acceptance of one's mistakes and striving to improve from experiences.

I

Babe, we were living at Bath
In those days
In the amphitheatre
Of the seven hills
Bathed in beauty!

In the elegant city
You narrated its history
The Romans built
A world heritage centre:
Royal baths, saunas
And plunge pools!

The Romans found the Celtic god
They started worshipping Sul
The Celt sun god

And the Roman god Minerva!
We walked along the arcades
Visiting the Roman baths
Museum, spa and pump room!

Walking along the tourist trails
Seeing the Georgian architecture
The King's Circus, Royal Crescent
Parade Garden, Pulteney Bridge
Along the banks of River Avon
Where once Agatha Christie
Charles Dickens, Jane Austen
Might have spent hours of their lives
Seeing the river Avon flowing!

2

That evening
Do you remember, my love
Awoke in the dusk
In a foul mood
Wind ran amuck
Down the Bath wick hills in Bath!

Roaring in fury was the storm
Drenched completely
Bashing trees wildly on the way
Smearing on ice granules all over!
Engaged him
In tough wrestling
With his love

River Avon!
Avon was enjoying flowing slow
Crawling calmly like a snake in the valley
Crazy blizzard was pushing her to flow fast
In the reverse direction, opposite to the current!

Mad was the cloud burst
Manhandled her the thunderstorm
Madly attacked her in the night
Brutally bruised quiet helpless River Avon!

Lost was her mental harmony
Determined not to lose her will
No way had she wanted
Any change in her ways!

3

That day there at Abbey
Down below the clock tower
Lost blissfully
In a timeless spaceless own world
A saxophonist poured his heart out
Shivering; in downpouring rain
Blasted by angry hail storm
Frozen in ice covered chillness
Collecting only ice granules
In his begging hat affront of him!

While hunger played its robust music
Well orchestrated inside his stomach
The saxophonist sang aloud

Fury of the Wind

Relentlessly:
'I loved you, my wife
And still love you, my honey
Forgive me if you can
The beast in me by now
Forget me not my baby!

Sorry for beating you mad
Assaulting you brutally
Torturing you mentally
And breaking our strong wedlock
In moments of lunatic temper!'

Irritated his dog too
In sheer bored of his music
It barked at him in anger
Ill tempered in hunger!

The saxophonist continued
Blowing his pained heart out
In rain, in snow, in hurricane
In regret, repenting in anguish
In blissful unawareness of himself
His dog and the world around him!

Poem-8

OUTSOURCING LOVE

Being female and male primordial energy forms, travelling in the speed of mind waves since the very beginning of the abyss, the Cosmic Womb, the couple Yin & Yang have been aware of what has been happening in the world since the very beginning, even before the human animals' interpretation of the Big Bang Theory of the origin of universe and origin of life!

While globetrotting, living in many of the cities, witnessing, observing, overseeing what is going on, the couple realizes that life is fast changing and wonder: Is outsourcing love fast becoming the buzz word not only in business but in love life too?

I

In a world where only
Money matters
Buzzword is outsourcing
Business of body, mind, intellect
Business of life, love and joy of living!
Engaging men, women
Transvestites and babies
Bundled or segregated
For time-sharing !

No space, no time
In life but for money !
Isn't love outsourcing
An offshoot of life?

Outsourcing Love

In the hurry worry
Hassles of modern life
We profess
The age old profession !

We have been there since ages
In Babylonia, Mesopotamia
Ancient Greece, Rome, India!

Ancient world knew
Bible, Koran talked about us
Wasn't there sacred marriage
Wasn't there 'offer' of us to Gods?
Women waited
In the temple of Aphrodite[1]
To have intercourse with stranger!

Money makes the act sacred
Never refused to any men to avert sin!
'Devadasis' the dancing girls who danced
In the temples of South India
Offered their body, dancing
Prohibited women and concubines
Traded, sold and leased their body for living
To the unfaithful, locked in wedlock!

Gigolos do pretty business too
Do the same thing we do
Escorting women
Hungry for man's flesh!

---
[1] the ancient Greek goddess of love and beauty, identified by the Romans with Venus.

2

We are 'unreal'
Partners but real
Wives, husbands
In the unreal but real!

We live in cities
Villages, everywhere
Outsourcing
Spouse's core services
Specializing
In servicing men and women
Our core competence is well known!

Who says gone are those days
Kings, emperors, queens
Who says the days are over
Harems, concubines
Dancing girls, Eunuchs
Not yet buried in history!

In this unreal world of the real
Or in the real world of the unreal
Men and women live in secrets
Ever loving men, women, children
Harems, concubines, Eunuchs!

We are lovers of everyone
Those who can afford
Need good tim
Living in love

With live robots
Paying for
Love machines!

We are for lovers
Of everyone
Those who lost freedom
Tired of the routine
The real, lusty, sexy
In-satiated beings
Of the unreal, bored of home!

3

Nay! We don't sell everything
May be body for living
What God has gifted
But not our mind
Soul, spirit and intellect!

Who knows, who cares
Name, emotions, feelings?
We keep away from the 'wolves'
Our life secure, sublime sacred
In churches, mosques
In temples, monasteries
In Gurudwara, synagogues
In the sanctum sanctorum
Of our unadulterated sublime mind!

Divine and pure is our heart
Filled in love, care, affection

To those whom we live
To those whom we love
To those whom we're
Renting and leasing our body!

We love our family
Love not this unjust
Loveless unequal
Duplicitous world!

We too need money
To live, love and take care
For whom we love!

We sell our body to 'wolves'
Let the hungry starved ones
Gobble the raw human flesh
Let them have our body for a price
Let those deceitful actors enjoy and have fun!

We know
He who knows
Forgive us
From the sin
Of this living
Of this loving!

We're everybody's love
For a price, for lease, for rent
That only matters in the 'real world'
Looking though like the unreal

Poem-9

DANGEROUS WORLD

Representing the energy vibes of the world, the couple, while circumambulating in the world in the speed of mind waves, faster than light waves, oversees the crime infested world.

They notice crime increases all over the world; especially those against hapless women and children. They feel something is to be done against the innovative crime scenario, reflecting decadence of the human values.

I

Travelling along the **NOIDA** roads in Delhi
Near the **man eater criminals'** den
Where a cannibal murdered children
In cold blood
Knew nobody how many lads
He consumed or not!

Even the cops knew not
Why they were murdered
For flesh ?
Sex ?
Organs ?
Or just the act of cruelty!

My driver cautioned me:
"It's a dangerous world

Life has no meaning!
But there's price for organs !

Rich are the poorest of the poor even
Richly rich possessing healthy organs!
Unsafe are they wandering on the road
May be kidnapped, killed for rich organs
It is NOIDA, Greater Delhi in India!"

2

Ghostly fables of cruelty are there everywhere
Innovate are the ways of crime !
Tourists in Goa got murdered
With organs missing
Floated in Ganges
The body of a newly recruited gym trainer
Missing were the vital organs
Police found fish had eaten!

Child got murdered
While father and mother sleeping !
Men befriended strangers
Made sick, caused hospitalization
For taking out organs!

Media reported
Girl got raped
By classmates in daylight !
A leader enjoyed the body
Of his party colleague till got bored;
Burned her then in charcoal fire

Like chicken legs and breasts!
Boyfriend videoed
Naked love acrobatics
With his girlfriend
MMS-ed for titillation and money!
Parents traded children
For slavery and prostitution!

   3

Incredible was
The life story of a cannibal
Hunted his prey through Internet
Chatting, friendship ended
Killed and ate him!

Girls wearing high heels
Got whipped in terrorists land!
Lips wearing lipstick
Got slit in terrorist country!
Paedophiles sucked
The tender lips of baby girls;
Like Dracula
Sucking blood of Lucy!

Punks and drug addicts
Of London, Paris, Amsterdam
Lived in a psychedelic world
Created by drugs, engaged
In sadomasochism, necrophilia
Somnophilia and what not!

Unbelievable are the stories of cruelty
Of the human animals'
Murder of humanism
Adding new hues to cruelty
Against men, women and children!

The horrible spectrum of crime
Has terrifying shades in blood
Can we do something to make
The animal in man human?

Poem-10

STREETS ARE OUR HOME

The couple notices the plight of the street children in the world. Their number is increasing in developing countries. Underprivileged children live, work and die on the streets without getting any social welfare or security of life.

Yin & Yang notice that what the street children possess is enviable - the joy of living.

I

Streets are our home
Sky is our roof
Endless roads are there
More than what we need !
We are gleeful with life
When life snarls at us

Born on the street
Living on pavements
Working, eating
Excreting and sleeping there!

Playing in the rain
In sun, day in and day out
Even dying on the streets
While fighting for living
We have nobody

But the Creator
Taking life on its horns!

2

Let me tell you
The story of my family
I'm a cursed tiny, bony
Pale, little, street lad
You can count my ribs!
I love my younger brother
And my youngest sister too!

We're richly rich kids
Own a plastic bottle of drain water
We want to bathe my pretty naughty baby sister!

We're good at acting
We play in this drama
Called life!
Our mom is a sole producer
A great director of this show!

'Run, catch her fast'
Mom directs my brother
Every day he catches my sister
Running while she is busy playing
Mom directs me to pour water over her
Brother is good at holding her tight
She resists boy-handling though!

Restless, impatient but happy
Our great mom is benign
Directing the bathing ceremony
Without fail in perfect coordination!

3

Who says it's the struggle called life
It's a never ending fun for us
It's great running around naked and free
Swimming in the open drain and in rain!

We enjoy playing this life game
With buffaloes, pigs and kids like us!
We're damn good workers
Working twenty four into seven or whole life:
Working for others who employ us for a rant

We clean car glasses at the signals
We sell balloons, artefacts, books, toys
We were taught which book sells who wrote them!
We're good at our profession too – begging!

We're bold to shoo away diseases
We're tough kids born on the streets
We're born out of the street drama called love
We're beautiful street kids born to live like animals!

We live in Mumbai
Homing happily us on the streets
Hosting the biggest slums in the world!

We don't have a slum to live
We don't dream or care for big things!

Grateful are we
God fearing are we
To the mighty big
Bad bosses ruling the streets!
For letting we live
Letting we sleep on pavements
With our pet street dogs!

We've more fun sometimes
Sleeping crawling in pipelines
If we don't get sleep at night
When road gets empty
We enjoy seeing
Mom and dad smiling
Whispering something really good!

4

Mom taught us
We've nothing to lose
And everything to gain
Nothing stops us owning
A slum in the days to come
Or becoming a big street boss
Or a slum dog billionaire!

Can anyone take away
The smile from our face

Come whatever may
It's the attitude that matters!
Can anyone delete
Destiny imprinted
By our doing or undoing
Or others doing or undoing
Being human is divine
Though all is not well for all!

Those all mighty Gods in life
May add, delete, subtract
Multiply, divide, doing away
Doing or undoing destiny
To make all is well for all!

We are grateful to Him
Keeping us alive
In this exciting drama called life
Gazing at life and death
In every moment
Its deadliest, terrific show!

We love life fresh and raw
You are merciful Lord
You love us
We have smiles!

You protect us
From the unknown

All mighty!
Taking away, our hunger
Pain, disease, worries
That is why we call you
The God Almighty!
The Super Duper Boss!

Poem-11

CHAMELEON WOMAN

While globetrotting the entire globe, Yin & Yang have been witnessing divergent life patterns in different developed and developing parts of the word, including malnourished, famine affected, starving millions of hapless victims of life in regions like Sub Saharan Africa.

While living in Delhi, the capital city in India, the couple experiences the horrible plight of street women in Delhi. They notice that what makes life worth living is probably accepting what is in store, understanding the hidden risks and opportunities and turn them into challenges and opportunities.

I

Attired in garish but torn sari
Concealing peeping out
Bulging, soft voluptuous
Curves of youth
Stood at the traffic signal
A street woman with babies
Selling:
Red, green, yellow balloons!

Screaming twin babies
One boy, the other girl
Clutching her firmly
One, on the left

The other on the right
Engaged in competition
Sucking mother's milk
From right at the source!

A chameleon woman she is
Changes appearance often!
Before the earliest bird
Chirrups at the day break
Holding babies close to bosom
With a big sack on her back
She searches rags, waste heaps
Something that fetches value!

Challenging pigs, dogs, cats, cattle
Rats and folks of her kind
Is the game she has been good at!
Managing thugs who allocate
Streets for begging
And for living for a price
Of course god is kind in his bounty!

She lives her life in love
Beneath a flyover in Delhi
Destined, born on the street
Cursed for others but blessed for her
She has no quarrel with the almighty
To be blossomed as a street girl
Pretty, colourful, alluring like a flower
Her hassles are with the all mighty!

2

Puberty brought
Its blues for her too
One wintry night
In deep slumber
Crawled into her blanket
A snake!

The crawling snake
Reused not to creep
Snaky licks, poor thing
Starved of food, hungry
Searching, coiling
Piercing, crushing
Tearing her apart
Devouring in greedy gulp
Like a hungry wolf on its prey!

While nauseating mixed odour
Of sweat, liquor, drugs, dirt, smoke
Penetrated into her nostrils;
She sensed the unruly whiskers pricking
Creeping and pouncing
From organ to organ!

Fast breaths
Buried in her ears
Aches, pain spread all over
She cursed the night

Her visitor too
He came to steal
Only what she had!
Gifting her
What she never wanted
But what the bastard believed in!

She cared little
No complaints
Life is as it comes for the poor
Visitors are welcome
Merrily, always thereafter!

3

Laws of the street are cruel
Under the rule of the jungle
Might is only right
There's no right to liberty
No freedom, or even right to life!

There's freedom on the street
To move anywhere along endlessly
From cities to cities to towns and villages
Begging, stealing at times!

Tough is the game of wrestling
With tough, rough, rogues
They're the bosses of the street
Sharing streets with the smart police!

Right to live is absolute on the streets
Till death encounters!
Who stops any way
A rag picker woman's babies
Becoming street dog
Millionaire?
Billionaire?
Or even zillionaire?

Poem-12

THIS DANCE IS OUR LIFE

Yin & Yang have been observing human life patterns in various parts of earth. They know human beings live in different ways with different social norms, ethical principles, ideals of life. Life in Amsterdam, Bangkok, Scandinavian countries, Africa, American continents is all different with different social norms and do's and don'ts.

The couple notices that life of the unfortunate people like Eunuchs (*Hijras*) in India is pathetic, horrible, humiliating and tragic. In the developed world, the transvestites are treated like any other citizens with same rights and responsibilities. They work in entertainment and sex industry. Their right to live, right to work and right to social security are recognized.

I

In swarm
They came
Like flies attracted by dirt
In search of food!

Drum beating began
Out of the blue
Accompanied by belly-beating
Hips gyrating, body vibrating
Howling, singing
Crooning, jumping

Shouting obscenities
At the top of their voice!

They danced
In tantrum exhibiting
Fried in scorching summer sun
Soaked in sweat and dust
Exhilarated expecting
In effervescence of joy
Celebrating the new birth!

They were large in number
Unwelcome
Draped in tattered skirts
With painted hollow cheeks
Mascara applied eyelashes
'Beedi'[1] smoked lips!

Street boys joined them
Teenagers peeped
Middle aged men got curious
They continued dancing
Making the show exciting!

2

"Let us inspect the newborn
It's our right to know
Is the baby a boy or a girl?
Or just like us! Our baby!

---

[1] cigarette made of tobacco flake wrapped in a tendu

Can't we take the baby with us
To bring up as our offspring
Destined to live
On this cursed dance lifelong?"

Through the front door of the flat
Crept in the leader of the clan
Inspected, muttered in despair:

"Okay, we agree
No dispute
Baby is a boy
And not ours!
But we'll celebrate
Till you give our fees!"

"Stop dancing, please
We had enough of it
We'll give your price
Won't you kindly
Please leave us alone?";
Begged the father of the newborn!

3

"You branded us as 'Hijras'
Ostracized us for lifelong
You hate us
Treat worse than mad dogs!

This un-rhythmic vulgar dance is our life
Our dance is for living

And this curse is our life
Destined to dance is our fate
We'll continue dancing
Whether you like it
Or you hate it!

Remember
We too have a right to live
We were born
Not out of our act!

Give us our fees
What is due to us
Let us rejoice
The new birth!

Let us celebrate
Singing and dancing
Let us share
Your happiness
And bless
The newborn child!"

Poem-13

MY HUBBY DEAR

The couple notices that there are people who over enjoy life having no control over their senses or desires, despite risky consequences. Nobody can help them but themselves. Nobody can dare to say the truth directly: how to make them realise to help themselves?

I

Treating own tummy like a waste bin
Gobbling everything come his way
Drinking liquor as elixir of life
Consuming his and others' share of food
Tummy lover my hubby dear
Grew big round and conspicuous!

His heart ached, pumping blood all over
Lungs worked hard to bring air in him
Kidneys, liver, pancreas worked overtime
Giving signs of giving in and worn out!

His spine bent, hips sagged, balancing the fat
Debauchery he loved food, liquor, vice, galore
Indulged in what he liked more and more

Money power made him stubborn like a stud
He felt great looking down upon others

Enjoyed life eating, drinking, merry making, partying
Having food, drink, fun, frolic, sex and what not!

Pot belly led him ahead always
He crawling behind like a penguin
Thin legs shrieked under the weight
Arched, trembled, struggled and pained
Carrying overweight at hips and above
Amazed was his doctor
How he carried him!

2

I love my hubby dear
Fat and ugly though
God give him sense
To take care of him

Let him eat enough
But let him leave food
That is not good for him
Food meant for others!

Lord, if you don't
Who'll instill
The fear of God?
Who'll control
Ever growing
Urge to eat?
Who'll make him manage
His ever demanding belly?

Won't you help him
Discipline his senses?
Lord, be kind
Give strength to his heart
Make him wise
Treating good with his organs!

I love my hubby dear
In the core of my heart
Make him happy lifelong!
Helpless am I
Controlling his urge to debauch
His irritation, ill temper,
Fretting and fuming!

I pray thee to help him
Make him healthy, safe and sound
In body, mind, spirits
Words, thought and action!

Poem-14
THE GYMNAST OF THE MIND

The couple visits Shravanabelagola in Karnataka, the pilgrimage centre for the Jains. They meet a saint in the forest.
They notice that mind gymnasium is equally important as building body. It helps to add beauty and stamina to mind and body to lead a healthy, happy, and satisfying life.

I
The fifty seven feet tall
Munificent, magnificent
Monolithic statue
Of Bhagwan Gomateshwara Bahubali
Of the tenth century statue
Stood naked in deep meditation
As a symbol of non-violence
And renunciation for centuries!
Nestled atop in the verdant
Chandragiri and Vindhyagiri Hills
In Karnataka at Shravanabelagola!

There Emperor Chandragupta
Meditated and Emperor Ashoka
Erected memorial in his memory
In the third century BC!

Babe, do you remember
We were there
At the Mahamasthakabhisheka
Witnessing the spectacular ceremony
Immersing the statue
In milk, curd, ghee, saffron
And offering gold coins aplenty!
The legendary seeker of truth
One of the twenty first saints of the Jains
Proving purity for soul, compassion and love!

2

We met the naked saint there
He lives in the forest
Wearing nothing
 But costume made of
Air, ether, space and sky!

His birthday suit gets fading
Wrinkling, being constantly used
Though it makes
No difference to his beautiful mind!

Great yogi he is
Living in harmony with nature
Brushes nothing
Bathes no body!
He combs no hair
He sees no mirror

He sees no barber
He shaves not!

He knows not
How he looks
His body is a stranger to him!

He loves
Mastering his senses
Like a snake charmer
Playing with his snakes
Not permitting
The snakes to poison him!

3

Children smile at him
Ladies feel shy seeing him
He withdraws at times
In his tortoise shell
Spending hours in silence
In union with the supreme bliss
In the ocean of his mind
Rediscovering him
Untouched, unspoilt
By the surroundings!

He sees him in others
Others are his mirror
He sees him reflected!
He is the source of love

Heals wounded hearts
Cures disturbed minds
Induces sense
In senseless brains!

He absorbs others' pain
Radiates only divine delight
He gives love to all
Absorbs pain and sorrow

He is the ultimate mind trainer
The gymnast of the mind
Who developed infinite packs
Of solid layers of muscles
On his beautiful mind!

Poem-15

WILD SPIDER IN THE SKY

The couple had a unique experience in an aircraft journey from Delhi to Mumbai. They notice that mind is the most powerful when the inner energy is identified, focussed and fully concentrated for problem resolution; connecting with the supreme positive energy flow in the universe. Optimising inner energy linking with the cosmic force may help in deriving optimum capacity in life threatening situations. This is a poetic version of what had actually happened.

I

Babe, didn't it happen
When we were in the sky
In the mid air
Flying in the super jet aircraft
While having sumptuous lunch in the air
In between the starting point
And the destination!

Suspended were we
In the stratosphere
When the pilot told:
"We are landing
The same place
We took off!"

Alarmed we looked
Knowing not
Hijacking, accident
Error in the engine?

Pink beautiful cheeks
Of the young air hostess smiled
Bringing the freshness of blooming roses

Her pretty lips
Painted in lovely red lipstick pursed
Pearl like white teeth sparkled:
"Don't you worry, madam
Just a small crack on the windshield!
You'll get connecting aircraft
To the destination!
Just relax!

We'll be there
At the starting place
Just in twenty minutes"

2

Wasn't it a microscopic point
Sharp pinpoint hole in front?
Right at the glass windshield
Right before the eyes
Staring straight at the pilot
Piercing through his eyes!

Poem-16

I DON'T REMEMBER

The couple notices that memories may fail, but reality remains. Mother's love is incomparable, may be comparable to the Mother Nature's love to human beings! Yang remembers in this poem how it is difficult to remember some of the best times of life in the beginning!

I don't remember
How as an embryo
I coexisted in the womb
Of my mother!

I don't remember
How I lived in her
Like a parasite sharing
Her Oxygen, nutrients, blood!

Soaked in her body fluid
Floated in her life giving nectar
Rocking in comfort
Kicking her in joy
Dreaming in bliss!

I don't remember
How I swam out of her womb

One day screaming
Pushing and tearing her apart!

Giving her the pain of being
Splitting into two beings
Wrapped in her placenta!

I don't remember
How I cried aloud frightened
Seeing the daylight brightened
In the hot dusty noisy world
Realizing being lonely naked!

I don't remember
How I grabbed her in panic
And held her tight
Fed my hungry belly
Quenched my thirsty tummy
Drinking pure milk from the best source!

I don't remember! I don't...
Nothing is clear in my misty cloudy mind!
But I do remember
When I was a child
When I could express
My feelings, emotions and fear
I asked my mother:
"Mom! If the sky crumbles
And falls down
On my head while playing

What'll I do?
Who'll take care of me?"

My mom hugged me
Close to her bosom and said:
"My Child! Don't you worry!
Never will the sky fall on you!

As long as I'm alive
I'm there to take care of you!
When I'm not there
The Almighty will take care of you!"

Poem-17

LIVING GREEN WITH NATURE

The couple celebrated their marriage anniversary in a tree house at eco resort in a wildlife sanctuary in Kerala. They loved living in nature and noticed that living in tune with nature is real bliss! In this poem, Darling narrates their experience in Wayanad!

I

Babe, do you remember
We were in the 'God's own country'
In Kerala at Wayanad
Jungle eco resort
In the pristine, wild
Virgin forest at Vythiri!

We were celebrating
Our marriage anniversary
In that romantic get-away
Tucked in the tummy of the hills
In a Tree House
Amidst the green leaves
Bordered by the animated
Live tropical rain forest
In exclusive seclusion
Running away from the human animals

The point stared at pilot straight
Grew bigger and bigger in diameter
Shattering the windshield glass
Showing an unruly, wicked
Gargantuan, deadly spider
Busily weaving rapidly its cobweb
In the air to trap its prey
Leaving no escape, with no fail!

To be or not to be
To live or not to live
To let or not to let
That's the question!

The rarefied air to suck
Shooting through the hole
Blasting him straight
Blowing him off
Bursting into fire balls!

Sucking him, his crew,
And the passengers
Into the rarefied
Dark hungry belly
Of the stratosphere!

3

The aircraft vibrated, violently wobbled
Moved up down vertically, horizontally
Curving, angling, diving, tilting
Cruised hurly burly, zigzag in turmoil

In turbulence, fully out of control
Evaluating, challenging, baffling
Terrifying the pilot and his avionic skills!

Terrified were we
Hearing the song of the child
In the backseat singing aloud laughing
Enjoying fully the roller coaster ride:
"Go up and down, jump and fly
Faster down, faster up
Faster, faster
My jerky jumpy jumbo jet!"

Experienced though
The Pilot knew not
How he trembled
Seeing straight
The watching
Third eye of Shiva
The eye that can fire
Inferno in moments!

Never ever did he
Encounter the uncontrollable
Never ever did
He experience
An aircraft rocking so wild
Participating in bizarre
Tumultuous cosmic dance!

4

Reverberated in his ear
The sound, fury, rhythm
Speed, force, the energy flow
The thundering steps
The Comic Dancer Shiva
Was dancing
The king of all dancers!

Meditated the pilot, focussing
The supreme energy vibes
Moved in tune
He knew he was in the dance!

Wasn't he linked into the loop
Of the supreme power in the moment
Wasn't he felt connected
Experiencing supreme energy flow
Manoeuvring the unruly aircraft
With the superhuman skill!

Wasn't it the spirit in him
Landed the aircraft safe
At the take off point?
When we landed
Didn't we see
The smashed windshield glass
Cracked like an automobile
Collided head on with one another?

Leaving strangely for unknown reason
A thin sheet in between
Still unbroken, resisting against
The rarefied stratosphere
Preventing the air cavity
From sucking everything in!

The thin line remained
In between life and death
Being and not being!
To be burst or not in the sky
Like a fire cracker with
A big bang!

Far, far away, hiding
From the hustling bustling humdrum!

2

We were breathless
Seduced endlessly
By the Princess Nature
Wearing ecstatic, esoteric lush pristine
Dark green pretty costume:
Brocaded by silver crystalline
Sparkling diamond waterfalls
Decorated by wild floral designs
Patented by the Almighty!

We were lost in ourselves
In the lap of the Princess Nature
Amidst the verdant valleys:
Listening to the lullabies
Of the bubbling streams
Warble of nightingales
Screaming peacocks
Hornbills, herons, egrets
Music of Magpie Robins, mynahs
Orchestrated by cooing of koels
Pecking of woodpeckers
Rustling grasses
Swaying bamboo trees!

3

Silence of the dark night was punctuated
By occasional trumpets of elephants

Growls of the tigers, barks of the jackals
Bellows of bulls, bells of deer, squeaks of rabbits!

In the midnight we woke up
Witnessing a tusker in musk
Hitting trees, breaking branches
Munching of leaves near the tree house
We embraced trembling out of fear
We knew the animal was angry and hungry
And we were guests in the animal house!

4

We trailed in the morning
The forest tracks on tamed pachyderm
Crossing the bushes of wild flowerbeds
Seeing flowers like butterflies flying all over!

We saw elephant herds
Grazing along grass fields
Lonely young tuskers
Enjoying having their way!

We knew not then the elephant saw
A bison charging towards it
It advanced trumpeting
Keeping its trunk high in the sky!

The mahout catapulted marbles
At the charging bison instantaneously
When wisdom prevailed in its head
The bison disappeared into the grass!

We were breathing in the un-smelt fragrance
Of the virgin green freshness of the wild
Hearing the unheard songs of the unseen birds
Cooing for its mates echoing in the green valleys!

5

When we went for the spa for a real treat
The instrumental music was playing slow
Aroma of the herbs flowed in the air
The therapist at the spa was busy
Entangled in the pulsating nerve ends!

The long experienced fingers
Dipped in warm medicated herbal oil
Busy in unlocking the knots and joints
Curled up in stress, jammed up in strain
On the back of our body along the spine!

6

We lived a week losing ourselves
Deep inside the wildlife sanctuary
Living in the habitat of animals and birds
Insects, butterflies, creatures and what not
Sharing their space, living in their home!

Amidst the green flora and fauna
 Seeing animals grazing
Flocking around, playing, relaxing
Mating, sleeping in front of the resort
Listening to birds' twittering

Strolling In and around
Living green with nature!

We lived amidst cheetah, tigers, deer
Wild elephant herds
Cubs, tuskers, porcupines, boars
Rabbits, jackals, bison
Snakes, birds, creatures, bees, butterflies
Trees, grass, bush, creepers, insects
Coexisting in the jungle around the resort
Close to the Mother Nature
In a live and let others live environ
Living purely on need
But not on greed!

7

Careful were we
Not to intrude too much in their life
Sensitive were we
Not to encroach
Too much of their space!

Didn't we feel then living
In one ecosystem together
With river, rocks, mountains
Forest, animals, and creatures!

Babe, didn't we forget
The maddening city

Living till then all along
Amidst the human animals
In jungles of concrete
Glass, cement, steel!

Stressed up were we
In a never ending race
With never ending desires
With never ending greed
We were chasing
Milestones and targets
Galloping like horses!

I remember
The Tolstoy story
You told
The man running
Sunrise to sunset
Owning land, till exhausted
Dying with no land!

Aren't we
In an overdrive,
In a crazy chase
Do or die
Do before die race
Unlike animals
Eating to live
Only when hungry!

Poem-18

I'M THE EMPEROR

The couple gets impressed by the Real Emperor attitude in an otherwise difficult abandoned life of a very old man living away from his family.

They notice that feeling rich in mind is not to show off! What matters is the feeling of being an emperor, because emperor can also feel like a beggar even after conquering the world and nothing stops a street beggar feeling great really like an emperor thinking that the whole world is his.

After experiencing varied life patterns in the world in the 'Spectrum of Life' the couple talks about a man who has cultivated the right attitude to life to enjoy and to have a beautiful mind!

Every day in the morning
He peeps into my bedroom
His warm hands stroke me
His long golden fingers
Massage my eyelids!

He opens my eyes softly
Just to see him smiling
And he makes me smile every day!
He is my son,
Your son
And our SUN!

I'm the Emperor

Fresh air from the park
Brings new life in me!
Ceaseless waves in the sea
Brings new hope!
Cock a doodle doo
Reminds me
To 'get ready'!
Birds tweet and twitter
Cheer me good morning!
Crows crowing tell me
Go for morning walk!

Parrots romance before me
Advising me to enjoy love!
Pigeons in pairs singing
The beauty of friendship!

I wake up every day
Feeling like a Roman emperor!
I feel I own the park
And the sea beyond!

Who says
The skyscrapers are not mine?
Even if I don't;
How does it matter?
Who can anyway take away
The pleasure of seeing the park
Or the joy of feeling
In me as if I own them?

The tennis players,
Morning joggers, body builders
Yoga students
Laughing club members
All perform
Make me feel great!

Who says
I am an invalid currency
A retired pensioner
An abandoned, senile
Sceptical, crazy old man
Who says I am rejected
Dejected and sad?
Who says I live all alone at home?
Who says my children are not with me?
They are too busy
To visit me even once in a year!

Who says
I don't have a companion?
Who says
Nobody takes care of me?

May be true
Nobody may know
If something happens to me
All of a sudden

If I fuse off
In the silence of a midnight
Or wakes not
At the cock a doodle doo

But, it is me
And my attitude alone
Can make
Or break
My day and night!

Night I go to bed
When my love winks at me
She fails not to embrace me
Close to her bosom in ecstasy

The man in me,
Though old, too gets excited
When my beloved
The beautiful Moon cuddles me
 Dipping my whole world
In her sexy smile!

Empowered I'm
In the bliss
I'm the emperor
Not even a king!

I conquer and own
This beautiful world
By my attitude
To life, love and bliss

Come on
Guys you dare?
I bet! Can you, people
Take away
The joy of living
From me?

Theme Two
RAINBOW OF LOVE

The rainbow hues of love are fascinating!

When love happens, heart, mind, intellect, senses interplay bringing subtle nuances of love.

We experience different dimensions of love from the childhood: feelings of paternity, maternity, fraternity, affection, compassion, friendship, passion, lust and numerous shades.

We feel the flow of transcendental energy when we love.

We feel the energy is getting transmitted in the air in mental vibes reaching the desired persons. We call it telepathy. Proof of energy flow of love is experience only.

Living without some form of love is not possible. The creator has made certain to instill this feeling in all living beings.

Pure unadulterated selfless love takes human beings to spiritual heights, adds lyrics, poetry, rhyme, music, melody, tunes, and rhythm to life.

When love gets into different phases, it may appear that love decays over time; its energy gets dissipated over events in life, but gradually matures to higher levels.

The Rainbow of love takes the reader to the fantasy world of romanticism with its multi hues, fragrance, rhythm, and deep impressions of the joy of being in love, gradually transcending to transcendental ethereal heights of spirituality – the bond between Atman or soul and Paramatman or the supreme energy flow in the universe.

Poem-19

LOVE GAMES ON THE VALENTINE DAY

Yin & Yang find that life has changed over the years since the days of Stone Age. Technology changed the way human animals love in the modern Internet world.

In the global networked village, the man and woman in Whispering Mind fall in love, separated by time, space, distance, and geographical dimensions.

They find Innovative ways to express the feeling in their hearts. The couple celebrates the Valentine Day with new love games.

I

Our hunt
To find the right partner
Mr Right and Ms Right
Ended in the cyber world
Googling over the net!

We searched the globe
Day in and day out
Web chatting
'Orkuting', Skyping
Blogging, 'Face Booking'
And Twittering!
Internet made us finally lovers
Though living

On the two sides of the globe!
I remember
It was our first V Day
The fourteenth of February
The Saint Valentine's Day
The first valentine in the world!

2

Babe, you told me
The story of the poor priest
Who was jailed
By the Roman Emperor
For the crime of trying
Converting the emperor
Into Christianity
Instead of being
Converted
Into Roman Paganism!

Wasn't it ironical
The saint fell in love in jail
Cured the blind daughter of his Jailor
Converted her
Into the religion of love!
Scribbled and sent the first valentine
"From your valentine"
To his valentine before death!

3

We were living then in two countries
Diametrically opposite on the globe

Separated by distance, space and time
Linked together only by the internet and mobile!
On that V Day
We switched on our laptop
Simultaneously with Data card
Webcam and Skype!

I was trying to locate your home
At Niagara on the Lake
And you were finding my domicile
In South Delhi near the Qutub Minar!
Both of us Googled Earth
And traversed in mind waves!

That day first time
I was wearing an Armani suit
You presented me
Using the Amazon dot com!

You were blushing
In the pink Tommy Hilfiger dress
With the diamond
Heart shaped pendant:
I purchased at E-Bay
And sent to you!

4

We started listening
To Kenny G for a while
Chatted, smiled, giggled
Laughed and sent kisses!

I heard you singing
For the first time that day
We danced and watched
Each other dancing!

You told you picked up yoga
Tai Chi and belly dancing
And feasted my eyes:
'Yogaing'
'Tai Ching'
And belly dancing!

Later we watched
The movie of your choice
On the big plasma TVs
In our home theatres;
Exchanging expert
Comments on every scene
While having popcorn
And Coke together!

5

After the movie
We went to dining rooms
You watched me
Sitting under the chandelier!

When I was seeing you
Smiling in candlelight
You Skyped me:
'Open the Red wine bottle!'

Let me borrow
The colours of the rainbow
To paint my lips to kiss you!

3
When rays of love pass
Through the prism of life
I saw love
Emerging in myriad hues!

I want to love you the best
In the fusion of all shades!
Like father's love to daughter
And daughter's love to father!
Like mother's love to son
And son's love to mother!
Like mother's love to daughter
And daughter's love to mother!
Like father's love to son
And son's love to father!

Like brother's love to sister
And a sister's love to brother!
Like brother's love to brother
And sister's love to sister!
Like boyfriend's love to girlfriend
Like a girlfriend's love to boyfriend!
Like a true friend loves
A true friend!

4

In the fusion of colours of love
Let me create a rainbow of love
Like violet, indigo, blue, green
Yellow, orange and red in light!

Let me merge all the colours of love
Let me get the supreme form of love
Let me respect, admire, adore, acknowledge
Let me worship, and love you crazy forever
Let me love you from the very core of my heart
Let you fill in my mind, brain, self, soul spirit forever!

Poem-21

THE RELIGION OF LOVE

Yin and Yang notice that love makes positive changes in life. It is a divine, transformative, all embracing feeling; which changes the perspective of life.

Yang shares his feelings of getting baptised into the religion of love and worshiping Yin as a goddess in the sanctum sanctorum of his mind's temple. Yang follows different religious rituals to do 'puja' or worship his love to get the bliss of pure love from his goddess of love.

I

Mind stood
Like an impenetrable fortress
Till that day
That moment in my life:
When you looked into my eyes first time
I felt love
Transmitting electrons into my being!

A shining star rose
In the mental horizon
And your beautiful smile
Brightened my sky!

Happiness spread
Like perfume in heavenly bliss
I kept my star close
To my heart secretly adoring!

Like an innocent little boy
My heart went on humming
I love you my star, though
The star is not mine alone!

Who can prevent me
Dreaming her to be mine?
Tell me Lord!
Do I really need to possess
The star to be in my mind
Giving infinite bliss of love?

2

Babe!
You baptised me
That day
Into the religion of love!
Blossomed
In the garden of my mind
A beautiful rose then
I remained
A proud gardener
Nurturing the solitary plant!

I Skyped you then:
'Please pour wine in the glass'!
Together we cheered
And tasted the wine!

Didn't I show you then
Our photos printed on the glass
And the heart shaped cookies
You baked for me and sent
And the New Year calendar
With our photos on each month?

You kept red roses, chocolates
Cakes, gifts I sent to you
Webcam caught you coy
Showing me everything!

While you thanked me
For the dress and pendant
I saw love glittering
Like diamond in your eyes!

6

After the dinner
We went to bedrooms
You showed the new designed
Night dress I sent to you
And hugged the big teddy bear
Rolling over your bed
And sent goodnight kisses
Plenty with zygomatic smiles!

In the next week
I gifted you me
In a surprise visit
Dumbfounded
Eyes wide opened
Breathless were you
Seeing your real teddy bear
Live in action before you!

We knew from experience
Meaning of what Desmond Morris
Researched and found
The human animal is indeed
An uninhibited naked ape
In his private life!

Poem-20

RAINBOW OF LOVE

Lovers notice that love has different colours and shades like rainbow. The rainbow hues of love are fascinating in its intensity, depth and quality. Intense love is the complete integration of physical, mental, emotional, intellectual, spiritual dimensions.

Here in this poem Yang wants to love Yin in the supreme form of love, merging all different shades to bring the ultimate fusion of feelings between the two life partners!

I

Love birds flock
Everywhere romancing
At Marine Drive, Juhu
Bandra beaches in Mumbai
Delhi parks, London pubs
In Paris, Amsterdam
Bangkok and elsewhere!

Like pairs of pigeons coo
Peck, and smooch on terraces
Like parrots play the games
Of love on the trees!

Like bulls at the middle
Of the road islands in India

Love cow friends
With fondness and affection!
Like peacocks show the best dance
To impress the peahens
The cupid games of love
Are played the world around!

Please let me learn
The games of love
To love you the best
In the ultimate form of love!

2

Let me borrow the hues
Of butterflies for attire!

Let me learn
The humming song
Of the honey bees to sing!

Let me practise
The gait of elephant
To add majesty to my walk!

Let me follow
Dancing of peacocks
To exhibit the best in me!

Let me absorb love
Reflected in the eyes
Of a deer
To make my eyes speak!

While fresh fragrance
Created waves in the wind
Your ethereal smile
Created fresh breeze in my mind!
Tsunamis never erupted thereafter
In the ocean depths of my mind!
Even live volcanoes became
Dormant in the higher peaks!

Illuminated that day
In the corridors of my mind
Series of luminescent lamps
Removing darkness of sorrows!

You filled in my mind
Joy of living
And hope for the future!
Powerful grace of optimism
Radiated like
An aura around me then!

3

You know, Babe
In the sanctum sanctorum
Of the temple of my mind
I worshipped you, offering flowers
To my beautiful goddess of love!
Installing you in my mind

Half of the **Ardhanareeshwara** idol
Joining me
The other half
without you knowing
Merging in you-
Shakti, the female half
With me, the male half-**Shiva!**
You know not
I became your **pujari**[1]
The priest in the temple
Of my mind!
Worshipping you,
My goddess!

I offered all pujas –
The religious rites I know
Doing **Aarati –**
Offering flowers
Delicacies, perfumes
And singing in praise of you!
Performing Abhishekam-
Pouring over milk, honey, ghee..'
Pushpanjali – offering flowers
Deeparadhana – lighting innumerable lamps
All rituals in the temple of my mind
Seeking the bliss of true love!

---

[1] priest

Reciting **Vedic** mantras
Performing rituals
Installing **Shrichakra**
And performing tantric
Buddhist rituals
All to please you!
Goddess of my love
You are always
In the core of my heart
In the temple of my mind
Blessing me with infinite bliss!

Poem-22

ENERGY FLOW OF LOVE

The couple knows that intense energy of genuine love elevates life to higher levels of spirituality. Sublime feelings of selflessness and oneness overpower the lovers' individual existence and connect them with the energy of love which is invisible like electricity or electromagnetism.

Yang shares his feelings of invisible but intense energy flow of love when he first meets Yin!

I

Away from the daily hassles
Under the green leaves of reverie
Pink flowers fell on my eyelids
Fragrance of you embraced me!

God gifted you beautiful eyes
Like windows of your mind
Looking deep into your pupil
I saw you capturing me in your camera!

Powerful were those eyes
Good to x-ray even heart and soul
Delving deep into your eyes
I was searching your soul!

Experiencing being entrapped
I was fathoming the depth of your mind
I knew I was losing my identity of being
While trying to merge in your Self!

I could sense
The eternal energy flow of love in me
That God gifted
To the living beings!

2

Gravitational force, we learnt
Electromagnetism, we understood
Flow of electrons protons, we studied
We knew not, till that day
The intense energy flow of love!

We knew, we were linked in a loop
Connected in waves of the energy
In an invisible zone of eternal bliss
Where time, space and existence got frozen
Mind, Soul, and Self got synchronized!

I felt my being
Got merged into your being
In bliss
We chanted the mantra
Hamsa – 'Who am I'?
Soham! Soham! Soham!

I am in You!
You are in Me!
We are part of Him!

   3

Let illusion and ignorance vanish!
Ego surrender before Super Ego!
Brahman, Atman are one and the same!
Ishvara and jiva are one and the same!
We are part of the Eternal life energy flow
We are part of the eternal world!

Where time and space get frozen
Mind, Soul, and Self get synchronized
We chanted: "Soham Brahmashri!"
'Tat Tvam Asi'

Thou art that
You are that!
That you are
I am that I am!
'Aham Brahmashmi!

Let us realize
Self is the reflection
Of the Ultimate Reality-Brahman!
Atman and Brahman are one and the same
When Brahman is without illusion
Atman is without ignorance, delusion and ego!

Let us merge our individuality
Into the supreme energy flow of the universe
Let us rejoice
In the bliss of sublime love!
Let us live like the two united in one
Let us be blessed
By the supreme joy of timeless bliss!

Poem-23

FRAGRANCE OF LOVE

Yin and Yang know that fragrance of love is ethereal when love is nurtured and selfless. Feeling of being in love is divine beyond time, space, selfishness and ego giving infinite bliss.

Yang experienced the fragrance of love when he first met Yin. He shares his inner feelings and notices that when selfishness poisons the relationship; love decays, crisis begins, taking away the joy of being cared and secure.

I

I saw a rose flower
Blossoming and smiling
On your dainty cheeks!
I breathed in
The fragrance:
A seed of emotion grew
In my mind
Like a rose plant!

I could hear, see, and smell
Touch, taste, and feel
The fragrance of love:
The pure, sublime love!
All my six senses got frozen

In a timeless, spaceless
Egoless amorous world!
Time flew away
In the speed of light
Hours of being with you
Left like a few moments
Seeing you too much
Became seeing you too little
More and more I loved you
The more and more the heart craved
I wish I could stop the clock
Be with you forever in love!

2

In the bliss of love
My being merged into yours
You existed for me
And I existed for you
And nothing mattered but you and me!

You lived for me
Caring me
You left you with me
To care you!

And I lived for you
Caring you
I left me with you
To care me!

In the invisible current of love
Selfish thoughts vanished
Love multiplied manifold
Love made life divine:
We felt near to the almighty;
Enjoying being secure!

3

Life flowed like a river
Taking twists, turns and deep cascades
Murky water ran down the hills
In spring, summer, autumn and winter!

When years rolled by
We forgot to care the rose plant
The magical plant
That brought fragrance in life

I find no smile
Of the rose in your cheeks
Busy lost in ourselves
Living only for self!

Emotions began
Stirring up
In the core of our hearts
Erupting volcanoes
With molten lava!

We forgot caring
Self focussed

Insecure, suspicious
Uncomfortable!

4

We knew, Babe
We had dumped love
Somewhere
In the course
Of the River of life!

Tell me, Honey
What's in a relationship
When we can't dissolve
You and me in us

The rose plant
Stopped flowering anymore
Bare thorns protrude
More than leaves

When'll the plant
Bear roses again
When'll the rose
Smile on your cheeks

When'll we experience
The ethereal smell
Dumbfounding
Irresistible
Scent of pure love!

Poem-24

MUSIC OF LOVE

Yang experiences intense music and orchestra in his heart when he first met Yin. He believes that when there is genuine love to a person, life becomes romantic with music, melody, rhyme and rhythm.

He knows that even the best expression of love in music, poetry, art, painting, sculpture is inadequate to capture love in its splendour.

Yang falls in the music of love and shares some of his inner feelings of being in love.

I

Babe
You bumped into me
Like a symphony
At Rhythm House
Searching for Beethoven
Mozart
Bach, Vivaldi —
The best of the classics!

Cool breeze
Brought your perfume
Black curly hair
Spread like clouds

Full moon face
Blossomed like lotus
The dimples
Couldn't hide your smile!

The anklets chimed
While you moved
A philharmonic orchestra
Began in my mind!

2

When you asked for
'The Joy of Man's Desiring'
I knew you could hear
The music in me!

When you smiled,
Giggled, laughed and talked
I was listening to
'The Four Seasons'!

When you talked
Looking into my eyes
I saw the 'Moonlight Sonata'
In front of me!

I was lost
In the heavenly music of your voice
Thinking of then
'The Marriage of Figaro'!

3

Later you used to sing
The best songs you knew
While I was resting my head
On your lap listening!

I used to compose
The best music for them
You used to correct
My inappropriate tunes!

You used to recite
The best poems I wrote
You used to correct
My incorrect rhymes!

I used to dance
To your tunes and melody
You used to correct
My rhythm and steps!

You only brought
Music and dance into our life
You only made
Rhymes in the poem of our life!

You composed
The best music for our love
You created new melody
Tune and fusion in our life!

4

You, know babe
The philharmonic orchestra
Begins even now
When you come home
From land beyond the seas

My love
Let me tell you a secret
In the theatre of my mind
You are the danseuse
Ever singing, dancing and rejoicing

You remain always
The symphony,
Rhythm, melody
The tune of life forever!

Poem-25

GOD IN THE HOLY CAVE

Babe and Darling went for trekking to the holy cave Amarnath in Kashmir. Darling shares their pilgrimage and intimate love story in this fable spiritual green poem on trekking to the Himalayan cave abode of Shiva and Shakti.

The couple wonders seeing the unique nature made ice Shivalinga waxing and waning in the lunar cycle. The journey to the cave is adventurous and risky, but spiritually elevating and rewarding. They are amazed at the natural beauty while clambering the Himalayan trails to the holy cave abode!

I

The Himalayas
The house of snows
The King of all mountains

Babe, don't you remember
Invited us once
To visit the God
In the Holy Cave!

Crossing over the meadows of gold
Beds of golden yellow flowers
Thick carpets of green
Trekking along
The nude mountains

Where once pine trees grew
And beyond where
Only rocks bloomed
In multi-hues!

Amidst the skeletons
Of naked groins of the mountains
We clambered along;
Hearing the music
Of bubbling waters of the stream
Down below, seeing
The dreadful crevices and the vale!

2

While scaling up the difficult terrains
We uttered the name of God
The pony riders were in glee
Fleecing disabled pilgrims
Taking for a ride
While their animals famished
Under the burden!

Meadows, flower beds, rivers
Valleys, hills, forests, lakes, glaciers
Trees, birds, animals
The diverse flora and fauna
Welcomed us showing the best
And taking us to the hidden cave!

'Sadhus' were everywhere
Both saintly and those fake ones

Some were fasting and chanting Mantras
Some practised begging profession!
Some mastered the art of cheating
Money was made
By **'Mantra' 'Tantra' 'Yantra' 'Puja'**[1]

Stories were told
Fables were concocted
Saintly deeds of Gods and Godmen
Played games on believers!

3

In the white glacier theatre of nature
Some mountains wept
Cried and melted in heat
Do you remember, my Babe
We saw **Amarganga** coming out
From the glacier womb of the Himalayas
Like nectar of ethereal bliss!

Smeared on ashes all over
Didn't we take a dip then
In the divine icy water?

When bone marrows seemed to freeze
Spirits warmed up in the belief
We felt we were getting connected
In a divine energy field unknown!
Having washed off sins
We scaled up the hill

---
[1] Worship

Searching the God in the Holy Cave
Reciting all the Vedic Mantras we knew
The hearts overflowing
In effervescence of joy!

We cared little
Whether Sadhus were real or fraud;
They cursed us or blessed us on the way:

We knew no pain
Experienced we
Only the divine energy flow!

4
The cave-home of Shiva and Shakti
Was hidden
In the groins
Inside bare skeleton mountains
In an inverted
Triangular opening
Of the womb of Mother Nature!

It was a full moon cycle
When ice **'shiva-linga'** grew full
We prayed
Before the glacier **linga**
Waxing and waning with lunar cycle:

We celebrated
The union of **Shiva Parvati;**
In **Ardhanareeshwara** form:
The union of nature **'Prakriti';**

With the Creator **'Purusha'**
Enjoyed pure bliss!
Perfect man woman union
The source of creative energy!

5

Do you remember, Babe
A **Sanyasi** blessed us and told:
"Blessed are those
Who come to **Amarnath**

Where the Creator
Revealed to his consort
The secret of creation
Of life in the universe!

Lying on his lap listening
To the Mantra for a while
Lord knew not, his consort
Parvati fell asleep

Listened to the story
By the pigeons in the cave
See, those immortal pigeons
Flying even now in the cave!";

Divine light awakened
In the Sanctum Sanctorum of our hearts
We continued meditation
Mind united in sublime ecstasy!

6

It snowed and snowed
On the way back home
We installed in our mind
The Abode of **Shiva Shakti**

Purified body and soul
Felt the warmth of love
God in the Holy Cave
Blessed us both

We knew not then
The seed of love
Was sown
In the fertile land!
God in the Holy cave
Gifted us the best gift of life
Made me a proud father
And you a proud mother

It is His magic spell
That we live in our offspring!
Prostrated before
The infinite energy of creation
Humbled by the mortality of the body

Knowing the immortality of the Atman
In an ever intensifying quench to realize
The true mission of the human life
Feeling heart full of compassion, love and gratitude
We fell asleep before the abode of God in us!

Poem-26

NEST BECOMES A CAGE

Yin and Yang were living in Delhi like two love birds. Yang became alone when Yin had to go abroad for sometime taking the baby bird along! In this green love poem, Yang experiences the pangs of being away from Yin and shares his feelings of anguish in the backdrop of pollution including noise pollution in Delhi.

I

On the banks of the Ocean of Noise
Traffic flew like turbulent rivers!
There we lived facing the **Sangam or union**;
Where mega Traffic Rivers intersected!

You told me:
"Don't you remember, my love?
Indus River and the mighty Ganges are in coition
Busy in procreation of the riotous monster baby
'The Ocean of Noise'"

I said:
"It mattered little
Whatever way you name
Those monstrous motor ways
Amazon! Nile!
Or Missouri Mississippi!

Never does it reduce
The deafening damn noise!"
We lived there
Like a pair of pigeons
Locked in love
Together with
The little chick
Making a nest
On the banks
Of the four way
Highway joint

Amidst noise
Dust, noxious fumes
Hiding behind
The green left of the trees
Witnessing the great
Confluence of the Rivers!

2

When you flapped
Your wings, flying away
Over the oceans
To the other side of the globe
Taking the chick along;

Leaving me
In search of the rays
Of new knowledge, new hope
To feel the Mother Earth the other side
To earn pounds, researching:

You know, my Babe
Our nest became a cage
Imprisoned me inside
All alone in anguish!

Deprived of your love
Our baby son's
Play and smiles
Sleeping with
Sweet memories at heart:

Haunted by thoughts
Disheartened, morose
I was down in the dumps;
Gazing at vacuum
Pouring out emotions
In hot springs of tears!

Immune to the wild roars
Of the wheeled monsters
Dashing along the traffic rivers
In the concrete jungle
Unaffected by heat, dust
Sound, rain, storm and sun
Insensitive to fumes excreted
By the automobiles
I remained like a statute
Fully blind, deaf and dumb!

3

A truck screeched
To halt in midnight
Before the signal
In an earth-quaking scream
I was awakened
Sweeping away the dam
Of the river of thoughts

Gushed through
Emotional torrents all of a sudden
Rolled down the mountains
Pebbles in my mind
Like the ceaseless
Traffic waves lashing outside!

The pangs of separation
Deepened
I cried aloud, broken hearted;
"Come back my dove
My woman, my lost rib
'Bone of my bones!
Flesh of my flesh'

I'm you – you're me
The other half
Let us live again
In the Garden of Eden
Like Adam and Eve

With two bodies and one soul
Like a pair of doves bonded in love
Cooing, wooing, chasing
And playing around

Come soon, my Sweetheart
Reconvert this cage
Into our dovecot
This prison
Into our sweet home!

Poem-27

THE GIFT FROM GOD

Yin & Yang know that child is a divine gift from nature, god or the supreme energy flow or consciousness! Nature or the Almighty is selective in his dispensation and not so kind to everyone. The couple notices that his reasons and logic are beyond the human mind.

I

Baby, when you came
From the other world
Like an angel
We were in the seventh heaven
In bliss
Blessed by the Almighty!

You came
After great expectation
In the thirteenth year of
Our love-locked life

Living with medicines
Therapies, surgery
Removing that grew
Giving birth to fibroids

Many a miscarriage
Bleeding, pain, aches
Mantra, tantra, puja, meditation
You arrived
Bringing joy unbound!

2

We rejoiced
Feeling proud
Though we didn't know
Why, how you came out of love
Nor did we know when, how and why
You chose to come at last
Transforming our frigid, fruitless life
Into a seventh heaven
Bringing spring
With flowers and fruits!

Seeing you
Took away all our worries
Hearing you
We felt the joy of living
Touching you
We experienced the divine
And playing with you
Brought the supreme bliss!

You replicated us
We knew not
How you did it
Synthesizing both energies

Of the mother and the father
Uniting the yin and yang in us!

3

You were the incarnation of love
The symbol of our union
Enduring endless turmoil
You were the gift from the God!

Baby, you made us wonder
You made us believe in us
You made us believe in God
You made us live in hope

You were the hope
You were our baby
The divine energy
Making difference in our lives
You're the gift from the Lord!

When you cried
Tear drops flew from our eyes
When you screamed in tantrum
We felt the stress and pain
Of the throbbing heart beats
When you desired
We strove wholeheartedly to fulfill
When you said something
We struggled hard to make it happen!

Baby, you linked us
With the divine inner energy

You connected us
With the cosmic vibration
You enchanted us
With the joy of living
You remained
Happiness embodied!

You're our reflection
Your mother and father in one
Containing our chromosomes
Our DNA, body cells
Blood, bone marrow
We were born again
We lived in ecstasy!

4

We prayed
You be happy ever
We wished
You be healthy forever
We urged
You be safe
Secure all time!

When you got sick
Fever caught us
Gave you the best medicines
The best doctors treated
You were operated
In the best hospital we knew

One night you told us
'Mom, Dad I've to go
He is right there calling me!'
Doctors continued administering
Medicines after tablets
Conducting tests after tests
Steadily sinking into coma
Flew away finally
Leaving us…

Abandoning abruptly
No reason; we knew
We knew not
What did we do
What made you
Leave us?

5

Like the great grandmother
The African black mother
Living in all human being
We used to dream
You would carry, us all along
Our genes, DNA, chromosome
Your dad, mom ad infinitum
From generations to generations
In life, energy, matter
Making us immortal
Part of the Brahman
The all pervading

Supreme energy!
Oh! Lord! Shivakameshvara!
The God who fulfills desires!
Why do you
Take away our daughter?
The offspring
You gifted us
Oh Lord!
What did we do
To get this punishment?

Poem-28

THE ZERO AND ONE LOVE STORY

In this poem Yin and Yang appear as Zero and One. Despite being intensely in love and knowing the philosophy of life, they slip into unknowingly delicate relationship hassles. In this poem the primordial female and male energy vibes enact the life drama for the benefit of others. Their quarrel accentuates into a sort of warfare!

They notice that while relationship crisis could be resolved using the behavioural theories pronounced in the book "I Am Ok! You Are Ok!"; the drama highlights critical ego clashes that may lead to major break up causes in married life!

Metaphysically the battle of Zero and One is the duality in creation, female male energy issue, the patriarchal and matriarchal rivalry for supremacy, the conflict between Yin and Yang, the Divine Mother and God Father, God Son and Holy Ghost!

I

May I tell you a story of the two
Zero and **One** are bosom friends
But they quarrelled off and on
To fight it out things unclear to them!

One morning **One** felt great
Provoked his friend **Zero**
Intoxicated by his big ego

Just after the morning cup of tea
Challenged **Zero** for a verbal duel:

"My dear friend **Zero**
I'm the **One**
That matters!

You're just a big **Zero**
You're nothing
A big vacuum!
You're hollow
'Emptiness beyond emptiness'!
You're the void
Abysmal depth
Absolute darkness!
A black hole!"

2

"My name is **Zero**
Not 'nothing'
I'm not hole
I'm the whole!

Mind you, I've value
More times than you
Keep me at the right side
I'll show you who am I!
Your value is the least
What the hell are you
Thinking of you?":

Retorted **Zero**
Shocked, in tears, heartbroken!

3

One withdrew a little
In his tortoise shell
But he continued arguing:
"May be true
The least value I have!"
Ha! Ha! He laughed:
"Your value is nothing!
Even less than me
Unless preceded by digits like me
You remain stupid!":
One shot
Point blank at **Zero**!

4

"May be true I'm **Not Ok**,
A zero in life, having no value
May be true, you're great
A hero going to conquer the world!

It is life: some are born like me
Poor, valueless for others!
Some are fortunate like you,
Born great! God knows why!"
Zero felt she is not ok
But one is ok!

5

"You're right **Zero**
I'm great, I'm good
I'm powerful I'm the thing
I'm muscled, mighty, strong
I'm a powerhouse of creation!

You're **Zero**,
Soft empty dark big hollow
Powerless, subdued
Withdrawn, bloody dark hole!

I want to show
How great I'm
I'll make everyone
To recognize me
All the zeroes like you
Will be ashamed
In this game of life
I want to win all the games solo"

Delighted **One**
Flew like a cock
Reached the rooftop to sing
His magnum opus-
A cock a doodle doo
Of his greatness!

6

Zero got agitated
Coughed out her venom:
"You are crazy **One**
The mischief maker
Why do you challenge me off and on?

The moment, you see me
You charge at me
Change your colour
Terrify me, you bull
Jumping at me
Pushing in my life
Pulling out of me
You bruise me
With your boorish brutish strokes!"
Boiling hot in temper
Zero caught **One**
Tight right on him!

7

"You may be anything
I don't care a damn
What matters to me
How well you treat me, you bum!

Your only hobby, I find
Showing me down
Making you feel great
Putting me down under your feet!

You're throwing stones
Like pebbles in the water
I have only nightmares
Of being with you!

I've even lost the power
Of dreaming something great
Don't ever attempt you goddamn **One**
Showing me never down again!

I warn you
I hate you
You bloody, get lost
You idiot from my life
And never ever
Show me off
Your wretched greatness!

If I'm nothing, remember
You aren't anything great
If I'm not Ok
You are not Ok too!

You are miserable
A human being
Condemnable
Incomplete like me!
Do you hear
The egoist
Quixotic; stupid
Dumb nincompoop of a man?"

Zero lambasted
The ballooned ego
Of **One** in red hot temper!

8

One became repentant:
"I'm nothing before you **Zero**
You're the primordial Mother Divine
The Cosmic womb
'The essence of the Almighty'
'Mother of God'
'Mother of Tao'
'Hokhmah'
'Matri Devi" Great Mother'
The symbol of Eternal Divine Mother!

You draw me towards your centre
Pull me inside the abysmal depth
You absorb me in full
Tempting me
Taking me deeper
Making me pusillanimous
Meek, weak and small
Throws me out enervated!"

The heart of **One** quaked
In the emotional tsunami
Voice choked, body trembled
He trembled in emotions!

9

One begged for apology
Tears rolled down
"**Zero**, my Darling
I'm sorry, my Love, my Life
You're my better half my Yin
How can I live without you?
I'm incomplete in your absence!

Separate we are
Zero and **one**
Powerless, purposeless
United we are complete whole
Powerful like Yin and Yang
Shiva Parvati in Ardhanareeshwara
United like in Shiva lingam
In the inverted
Central triangle of Shrichakra
Like negative and positive energy flow
Like north and south poles!

If I am One
You are Zero
I'll keep you
On my right
And we'll make ten!

You're not empty hole
But the crucible of creation
I'm just a grinding stone

We're like the switch off
And switch on position of light

You're not nothing
You're the female energy
Yin, Shakti, Eve.
Prakriti, Radha
The symbol of God Mother!

I'm the masculine energy
Yang, Shiva, Adam,
Purusha, Krishna
The symbol of God Father!

Together we make
The Cosmic Womb
Together we make
Day and night
Form action and reaction
Make thesis
And antithesis
Finding synthesis in union!

United we create
The Supreme Energy Flow
Brahman –
In the universe!"

10
"My darling **One**
Let me now tell you the truth

I am the absolute emptiness,
The abyss
Matrix, the Great Mother,
The ultimate reality!

I'm the first
I'm the last too
I'm the honoured and scorned abyss!

I'm the whore and I'm the virgin!
I'm the wife!
The holy sacred divine mother!
And the daughter too!

I'm knowledge, wisdom, bliss!
I'm also ignorance, darkness, abyss!

I'm strength!
I'm fear!
I'm the Thee!
The thought that dwells in light!

I was there before all
I live in every living
I'm the invisible
The one living in every creature!

I'm OM
The God that made you
And placed you

In your mother's womb
In the Garden of Eden!"

11

After the big sermon-
A verbal duel
The battle of emotions
Subsided in tranquillity
Who's bigger riddle ended
In **I am ok and you are also ok** song!

Lake in the mind
Remained calm without pebbles
Zero hugged **One**:
Felt warm and comfy!

He kissed and loved his friend
United in each other's care
The couple felt complete
Perfect, content, happy
Just like made for each other
By the great Maker!

Poem-29

IT RAINED IN MY MIND

The Zero and One battle skirmishes settle down but Yin had to leave Yang that day due to life's compelling circumstances. Yang expresses his pang of sorrow and anguish.

He experiences that heavy rains outside bring torrential downpour in his mind, intensifying the pain of loneliness and pang of separation. Yang finally finds a way out to get away from the pain and shares how true knowledge of life helps bringing peace in mind in such circumstances.

I

Lonely lost at home
In the evenings
I saw sea roaring
The Sun red with anger!

Mind whispered:
'Forgive me!
Forget me not'
Thoughts wandered
Like clouds in the sky
Before torrential rainfall
In the monsoon!

Heart ached
With pangs of separation
Clouds brought rain
Sea got agitated more!

Waves of emotions
Crashed on the shore
Life rolled into
Bundles of memory
Feelings melt
Into a few drops of tears!

Why was the sea
So turbulent?
Thunder roaring?
Was nature weeping?
Rain losing its rhythm?

2

Babe you left me
Alone that evening
Throwing the red Sun
Drowning in the sea!

Clouds lost direction
In the blind dark night
Moved hither thither
Collided one another!

It rained in my mind
Cats and dogs
Poured and poured
Melting my heart into tears!

3

The Sun rose
In the next day
In the horizon
Of my mind
Chariots of thoughts
Drove along
In the vast sky!

I witnessed the games
Of uninvited guests
I stopped the thoughts
Hijacking my aircrafts!

4

Twilight brought
The Moon with stars smiling!
In the river of thoughts
Let me start sailing
Safe in my boat
Away from the entangling
Whirlpools of desires!

Let me search
The Ocean
Of the Supreme Consciousness

Call it escapism
Detachment, selfishness
'Moksha' 'Fana' the nothingness
Dissolution, merger, the ultimate bliss!

May the Atman
Surrender before Thee
Merge into benign
Supreme energy flow!

May the **Jivatma**
Merge in to **Paramatma**
The very supreme absolute truth!

Let the Almighty protect us both
May we derive strength
From true knowledge
May there be perfect peace!

"May He protect both of us
May He nourish both of us
May we both acquire the capacity
May our study be brilliant
May we not argue with each other
Om peace, peace, peace"!

5

"Om Sahana Vavatu Sahanau Bhunaktu
Sahaveeryam Karavavahai
Tejas Vinavati Tamastuma Vidhwishavahai
Om Shantih Shantih Shantih!"

Poem-30

STORY OF LOVE AND ENVY

Yin and Yang have been observing the interplay, rivalry and war between love and envy since the biblical days or rather from the beginning of the world. They faced the bitter truth after leaving the Garden of Eden and lived like any family with children. They notice that the story of Love and Envy is the eternal story of good and evil. Envy ends when love is born. Love comes out when envy ends.

Love was born
Innocent out of love
By love for love
Knew only to love!

Envy was born
Crooked, guilty
Out of envy
By envy, for envy
Knew only to envy!

In the sky
Of the mind
While playing
Kites in the sky
Envy met
Love first

Started envying
How Love
Flies kites so high
And how me Envy
Flies so low!

Love started working on
How to help Envy
Flying kites
So high in the sky!

Envy saw Love
Second time
On the sea shore
Meditating in love
Unaware of stinging
Of a crab on the foot

Envy chased to kill the crab
Love put the crab into the water
Said to Envy:
'Envy, my friend
Be kind to the poor crab
Stinging is what crab is born for
But killing is not what
Human beings are born for!"

Envy liked envying ever
How the hell
Love grew so great!

When Love achieved something
Envy only envied what was in it?

Whenever Envy made
Not something
Love backed Envy
To make it happen!

Love felt rich
Having nothing but love
Ever smiled grateful
For having a friend in Envy!

Envy felt poor
Having everything but love
Envy was suspicious
Love liked others more
Became vindictive
Frowned ever, hated Love!

While Love was embracing
Envy killed Love
In cold blood
Like Cain butchered
His brother Abel
Green with jealousy
To rule in the sky
Of mind ever!

Envy knew not
The seed of Love

Started growing
In her to be reborn
As little cute baby
Resembling Love!

Poem-31

LOST LULLABY

In the course of drama of life, Yang was living alone now after Yin had to go for a while away from him due to life's compelling circumstances. He comes across sleeplessness many times at night. He feels that the best medicine for insomnia could be listening to the mother's lullaby, lying on her lap! He is trying to get rid of insomnia, forgetting the anxiety of being alone in life journey.

I

God of love **Kama**
Plays the game of love
Catches me unaware
All of a sudden
Starts dancing in the mind
With his consort **Rati**

Arrows of flowers
Bring irresistible desires
Of joy, attraction, infatuation
Sadness and pang of love!

Cupid and **Eros**
Join the alluring game
Desires start pulling
Strings of the violin

Lost Lullaby

Called mind
Music of pleasure and pain
Played on and on!

Goddess of **Nix**
Spreads her dark wings
At night
Goddess of sleep
Plays hide and seek game
God of **Hypnos**
Refuses to put my eyes to sleep
How can Morpheus come
To bless me with dreams?

2

When insomnia catches me
Unaware night after night
How can I woo Hypnos
To come back to my life?

How'll I hug him passionately
Close to my bosom?
How'll I fall in love
With him and be on the bed?
Help me **Zeus**
My life is difficult without him!

Battles and battles of thoughts
Go on and on
In the battlefield of mind!
Wars are fought, some won, and some lost

Who wants battles and wars all the time?
Peace is not there
Anywhere in the field
When will there be
End of all the wars
When will the war field
Of the mind be at ease?

Lullaby of the mother
Lost somewhere
In the abyss
Of the subconscious mind
Who will sing a lullaby
To an adult?
So let me find
A lullaby in me for sleeping!

3

Let me be on the lap
Of the Mother Nature
Let me listen to the Mother Nature
Let me put my body
From toe to head to rest
Let me relax
My nerves, muscles, and body!

Let me listen to the body clock ticking
Let me listen to the music of my heartbeats
Let me traverse with the flow of my breath
Let me focus on the sixth eye between the eyebrows

Lost Lullaby

Let me see the divine light inside the sixth chakra
Let me await the Goddess of Sleep to arrive
Let me await her to keep my eyes closed
Let me await her to cuddle me with love!

Poem-32

SAND DUNES OF TIME

Living alone, Yang remembers how life has slipped away like sand particles under the feet in the waves on the sea shore. In the backdrop of Sand Dunes of Sam, Yang connects his life threads to derive further strength to go ahead. Yang knows the eternal truth of the immortality of the soul in the real world but realization of time machine ticking in the so called unreal but look like real world makes him a little nostalgic about life gone by. The folk music flowing in the desert in dusk pulls strings of emotions in the music instrument like his mind!

I

In the midst of the Thar desert
At Sam Sand Dunes
Of Jaisalmer in Rajasthan:
Shifting sandstorms form sand hills
Blocking roads, burying animals and people
Creating fast changing laid back desert wrinkles!

In the whirling air currents
In the shifting changing patterns
In the magic of sweeping dunes and vibes
Babe, do you remember
We rode over the breathtaking
Crests and troughs of sand hills!

In the romance of the solitude
In the fairyland of blasting waves of sand
We reached the desert safari camp
In the crimson glow of the setting sun
Riding on a camel caravan!

How can I forget?
Tell me babe, can you?
I remember you were smiling all the way
While irritated eyes brought sand particles in tears!

In the heart caressing folk music
Ballads of romances of passionate love
In the sound of the anklets of the dancing girls
In the crimson twilight, in the rhythm and rhyme
We were lost in dust, sand, sound of camel races!
Puppet shows, music, folk dances, songs continued
The grand old desert festival was in its full bloom!

2

Shifting sand dunes
Shuffled patterns in the wind
The Thar Desert became alive
In the dusk before the sun set!

The folk music continued flowing
Ballads of the legendary lovers
Swept in the wind
Making patterns in the mind!
In the faint orange glow of the log fire
Emotions outpoured in the twilight

Pulled strings of music in my heart!
Babe, I was rolling down
In the sand dunes
Like a dog in frenzy or an adamant little boy
Along with of course our little son
The sweet gift from the Almighty
Faster and faster he rolled down
I followed as fast as I could!

You were always acting as referee
Deciding all the matches against me in life
To my utter frustration of doing good before too late
Just to please the little fast growing sweet gift from the god!

The child in me laughed: Ha! Ha! Ha!
The adult in me questioned: What a fun?
Father in me cautioned: Be careful
The man in me got tired: Oh! Oops!

The competitor in me
Became green with envy
Babe, you remained calm
Being always a one sided referee
Taking no cognizance
Of any of my complaints!

We sat in the open air restaurant
In the desert safari camp
Tasting the thick strange camel milk tea
We were seeing the glow in the face

Of the desert goddess in the campfire!
In the star studded night
Later In the open air
Seeing the sky
Under the sky
We slept
Breathing in the desert air!

3

Years rolled by
Life moved ahead
Time leaving its
Indelible deep imprints
In every part, cell and organ
Of the body machine:
Beyond the cosmetic jugglery
And servicing and repair!

Now, babe
May I lay down
Under the sand dunes of time!
I remember
How time has slipped away
Like sand particles slipping away
Under the feet in the waves in the sea shore!

Years find our gift from the god
The boy growing as a man!
Years find the man aging old
Though mind refuses to age

We remain eternally fresh
Yin and Yang in our life forever!
What all happened in life
Remain now just as memories
What is aspired now
Yet to happen too
Remain just as dreams!

What all happened
Remain now like unreal
As if never happened
In memories in time;
Difference becomes thin!

Dreams realised
And dreams to be realised!
Events happened
And events to happen
Remain the same
Difference vanishes in time!
 Events fade into memories
And come in dreams
'The child is the father of man'!

Poem-33

TWILIGHT NOT MERGING INTO NIGHT

In spite of knowing the eternal truth of indestructibility of matter and energy, Yin & Yang realise that the time clock hung in the heart by the Maker of life, fades into disuse in the years to come.

In the course of the River of Life, Yang loses someone dear to him, his creator in a way. He misses the physical form of the matter and tries to find the presence of the indestructible energy vibes in the moving white clouds. Yang shares his thoughts through this self help philosophical imagery verses. He believes in looking for dear lost ones in the energy flow and having a healthy, inspiring, motivational dialogue. He engages his mind in hallucination and tries to look for the dear one even in moving cloud formations and get inspired, letting life going ahead.

I

It was an endless evening
Not merging into night
The aircraft from Los Angeles to Heathrow
Flew like an eagle
Against the spin of the Mother Earth
Suspending the twilight
Not vanishing into darkness!

Busy as usual
God was painting in the skies

Making abstract fast moving changing images
Brushing with saffron, golden, orange hues!

2

I was trying to interpret
The Almighty's live paintings:
Dark dragons crawling
Spitting fire from their mouth!
Hills, mountains, valleys
Moving cloud peaks
Constantly forming and reforming
Symbols and figures!

The herds of sheep formed in
Wandering dark clouds
Continued grazing
In the meadows of the sky!

3

You know, Dad!
In the sky, over the silver clouds
In those fast changing
Moving figures created by clouds
I figured you out
To have a friendly dad lad chat!

Dad, you waited for me
To come from the land beyond the seas
At the hospital bed you last laid
Before you left for the ICU!

You held my hand tight
Seeking assurance:
"I've waited all the time
For you to come, my son
I'm going; please take care
Your mom:
She has no one but you!"

When I see you moving in the sky
Metamorphosing into clouds
Goose pimples come over my body
Hairs stand still all over
In the roaring aircraft propeller's sound, Dad
I was trying to listen to the words of your wisdom!

I know you left the body
When it couldn't hold the soul
You abandoned the forlorn cloth
Liberating from the bondage
You're with me, I see you, hear you
And feel your presence!
I will always keep you with me
I need your love and blessings!

Poem-34

YOU BE YOUR MOM YOU BE YOUR BABY

Yang faces life as it comes. He believes in floating like a cloud in the mind sky and moving in the direction of wind without resisting. Yang being away from Yin, and after losing his father finds new inner principles to cheer him up! Though making money has never been a goal in his life, he has to accept that as fact of life.

The River of Life has taken Yang to meander in the oil rich desert, away from Yin and other loved ones in the city of Kuwait. Only passion in him is now to earn for the loved ones! Yang knows that living alone becomes unavoidable in modern life due to pressing reasons. He notices that nobody knows his needs, aspirations, feelings more than him. He wants to be his own mom in the desert giving mother's affection and desires to be his beloved too to love him and care him!

I

I was lost in the north east
Of the Arabian Peninsula;
In the west Asia, bordered by
Saudi Arabia, Iraq and the Persian Gulf:
In Kuwait – in the fortress built near water
The ancient Parthian port of trade
Between Mesopotamia and India!
The emirates were rebuilt from ashes
Where oil wells were set ablaze

By the retreating army
Creating environmental catastrophe
Destroying economic prosperity
Disturbing society, life, culture
Destabilising security of life and property!

My eyes were lost in viewing
The expanse of the Persian gulf:
Sitting silently sipping chilled water
In the viewing sphere
At the Kuwait towers
My mind is lost dreaming
The black gold in the wells!

2

Living in all alone in distant land
Leaving the sweet home away
Leaving the loved ones away
No one close to share
Heart, feelings, and emotions:

Money becomes the need
Money becomes the reality
Money becomes the mission
Money becomes the God
Making the ends meet!

Only God becomes Dollar
Pound, Euro, and Dinar
Helping meeting
Needs of the loved ones!

I don't see my mom
I don't see my dad
I don't see my beloved
I don't see my baby
Son, daughter, sister
Brother, and dear friends!

Distance does not mind
What matters is money
Who wants me minus money?
Money minus me is fine for whom?

Money becomes the goal
Only own shadows escort
Share moments of life
In the four walls of home
Chasing and being chased!

3

Mind whispers
"Be your mom!
Be your baby!
Be your dad!
Be your son!
Be your wife!
Be your husband!
Be your love!
Be everyone dear to you!
Play all the roles you like
The way you need

The way you like
And who
You want to be around
And how
You want to be greeted
How you want to be pampered and loved"?

You feed you! Your baby
Cheer up! Take care!
Who can take care?
You! Your baby!
More than You!
Your mom?

You were good
You're good
And you'll be good
Always for you!

Treat me well
Look me after
I love myself
If I don't care
Who can?
And who'll?
When I'm alone
In this desert land of wealth!

Poem-35

LIVING IN NOW

Yin & Yang know the power of celebrating NOW. The joy of life is living in NOW, not shadowed by the past and influenced by the anxieties of the future! Yang finds different ways of finding happiness in his lonely life, especially after Yin had to work at a different place away from him and he had to face life all alone. He shares his thoughts and philosophy as has been all along his wont in life with his beloved. He narrates how he wants to celebrate living in NOW with his formula.

I

I want to live in **now**
In the moment **now** ticks in
I want to rejoice, enjoy, celebrate
This moment of **now** in my life!

Let me breathe in **now**
Pure sublime air of life!
Let my lungs, heart, arteries
Veins and all cells of my body
Be rejuvenated by the Oxygen of life!

Let me forget my sorrows
Let me get out of my anguish
Let me forgive those who hurt me
Let me let loose me!

Let me let it go
Let me get lost in the sky
Like a freed bird from the cage
Let me afloat like a white cloud
Let me move in the sky of my mind
In the flow, in the wind, in the current!

2

I don't want to be a donkey for ever
Carrying others' burden on my back!
I don't want to carry anymore baggage
Those accumulated over the years
Decadent garbage of contaminated
Puerile, diseased human relationships
Painful memories, heart piercing thoughts!

I don't want to live
With the debits and credits
Drawing balance sheets of life
With plus and minus
Good deeds and bad deeds
Accumulated feelings and pains
Of those who impacted me and went by!

Let me be unchained
Let me unlock me free
From the chains and bondage
Of born and acquired relationships
Let me be free like a butterfly
Let me be like a grasshopper
Hopping in and out of happiness

Let me be a honey bee
Singing and humming in joy!

3

I know I can switch on
The dance of bliss in any moment!
When somebody or anybody
Dares or tries to take away the joy of my **now**
I will be in **now** rejoicing **now**
Celebrating joy of being in **now**
Letting my mind dancing in bliss!

Let me be detached
Let me be feeling liberated
Lord, let me celebrate this moment
Before it slips away
Let me live in **now**
Not tainted by the past
Not shadowed by the future
Let me rejoice and enjoy
Let me drink the nectar
The elixir of life to the fill!

Poem-36

JAI HO MY WEB OF LIFE

Yin & Yang were in San Francisco! They notice that life has been fast changing. Web of life has become the omniscient, omnipresent, omnipotent Almighty. All attributes of the Almighty can be found in the Web!

I

We were there in the high tech hub
In the capital of the Silicon Valley
In the southern part
Of the San Francisco Bay Area
The valley that led the list of patents
The city of Apple, EBay, Google, Hewlett
Yahoo, Adobe, Oracle, McAfee, Cisco!

When the centre of the dot com bubble
Burst in the NASDAQ stock market
In the city of micro chips
In the land of the venture capitalists:
The information technology wiz-kids
Experts in radio, television, electronics
Techies of Stanford, San Jose Universities
All creative minds are engineering for the future
Sleepless in the Silicon Valley of San Francisco!

2

Babe, you left me
In the darkness
In midnight
While sleeping
In our bedroom!

I didn't know
Were you so disheartened
Sitting all alone at night
In your study room weeping
Not knowing about
The illness growing in you!

Engrossed in
Chatting with those souls
Finding causes for...
Prescriptions, medicines
Analyzing causes, symptoms
Research findings for the problem...
Weren't you consulting them
Or praying to the new Almighty?

3

I know
You're hooked beyond control
Addicted to the charm of your friends
Those faceless souls!

Getting attached to them
More and more...
Being linked
Addicted to them
More and more...
Lives, brains, minds, beings...
Round the clock, obsessed
In sharing emotions
Feelings, pains
Joys, smiles and tears!

You are interconnected
With those faceless people
Whom I never saw or heard
Beyond space, time, region
With no qualms whatsoever!

4

Sorry, babe
Why do I blame you?
I confess
I'm also connected
Sharing intimate moments
The secrets
That I never revealed to you
Exploring to find more and more...
To be with those folks
In privacy sharing thoughts
Indulging fully in secrecy
Music, songs and humour

Fun, frolic, love
Spending many sleepless
Late night hours!

5

Babe, aren't you
And me only addicted to them?
Nay, even those smart guys are hooked
They make big money
In partnership
In collusion
While sipping scotch on rocks
Hacking and cracking
Beyond the borders
Making business
Out of drugs, sex, and terrorism!

6

These people are there
Everywhere, ever waiting
Scattered all along the planet
Hooked on tirelessly I
Looking forward to victims
Giving help, consulting, diagnosing
Expanding knowledge and wisdom
Beyond the frontiers
Towards the new horizons!

We are connected
Getting addicted more and more

Round the clock
Round the year, all along life
Ever transmitting
Telecasting, broadcasting...
Transporting, importing, exporting...
In an ever expanding world
Of rapidly growing power!

Helplessly hooked on to
The international information highway
Creating, redefining, researching
Ceaselessly expanding power
Of creation, preservation and destruction!

7

Hey!
My Web of Life!
Jai Ho!
Aren't you the new Almighty
The omniscient, omnipresent, omnipotent?
The collective wisdom of the humanity
The supreme consciousness
The divinity in the human being!

Let me Google
Let me Yahoo
And let me twitter
Let me Face-book!

I'm hooked
My family is hooked
The whole humanity
Is getting hooked
You're great WWW!
You are hugging everyone
Into your Web of life!

Theme Three:
JOURNEY TO INFINITE BLISS

Poems in this section are basically spiritual, philosophical and theological in content, but presented in simple, easy to understand verses bringing freshness and new romanticism. The idea is to expose the readers to some of the beautiful concepts on the secrets of creation of the living and the universe along with some benchmarked principles on life contained in the treasure house of human knowledge and wisdom, spread across different religions over many centuries, inherited by humanity from generations to generations.

The journey to bliss starts with a green poem on trees growing on temple, an icon for ecological balance and sustainable environment. The journey of life takes us to Bodhgaya, the place where Buddha got enlightenment. We move gradually learning the role of destiny and determinism in life towards improving the joy of living.

The fundamental quest to understand the purpose of life takes us to the process of self discovery through various meditation practices and techniques, metaphysical and ontological teachings of Buddhism, Hinduism, Sufism explained through symbols, icons, fables, anecdotes, Mantra, Tantra, myths and mythology.

In order to reach self actualization, it becomes inevitable to cleansing and churning of mind through easy to follow path of meditation, self discovery and thereby deriving true delight in living. Purification of thought process brings qualitative change in life perspectives and thereby help to reach the ultimate objective of the journey-the infinite bliss.

Poem-37

TREES IN TEMPLE

Yang is living alone away from Yin now days. He visits religious places to find solace in mind. His pilgrimage starts from visiting a peculiar tree temple in Cambodia.

Yin & Yang have been watching the human animal and finding that in the pursuit of satiating ever expanding greed for more and more of everything, human beings disturb the delicate balance of nature. Yang is not happy seeing the human animal taking too much risk of irritating his tolerant Mother Nature beyond the limits of her survival.

I

Babe
See in the womb of the temple
A tree is born!
The tree gives the womb
More seeds!
The womb gives birth
More baby trees!

The trees of Ta Prohm
At Angkor Wat
Grow out of the temple towers!
The temple walls crumble down
The roots of the fir

And silk cotton trees
Penetrate deep
Into the walls:
But hold
The crumbling stones of the temple!

2

Do the trees destroy the temple?
Or protect the temple?
The devotees go around wondering
But nobody knows
Nor can anyone guess the truth!

The temple and trees
Intermingle
Live in each other
And letting each other live too
Seeing is believing!

Trees grow
Grabbing the walls
Live in harmony
Making space for each other!

It pleases
The silent ancient God too
Who resides immortal
In the temple!

3

The crumbling temple
In the forest
Stands witnessing
The ever expanding greed
Of the human animals
In changing
Ecology and environment!

On Planet Earth
Where man is at war
With his benevolent
Mother Nature herself!

The temple onlooks
The deteriorating surroundings
Polluting air, water, biodiversity
Creating waste lands everywhere
Destroying the greens
Of pulsating lives!

Man infects Mother Nature
Forces her to inhale
Noxious Green House Gas fumes
Giving her influenza
With abnormally high temperature
Not treating her fast
With right medicines
Leaving her to fate
Doubtful for survival!

The tree temple
Stands alone
As a symbol of coexistence
Mutual dependence
Help and care
Teaching people
To live and let live
In mutual trust and care!

Isn't the world
Rapidly becoming unsustainable
In the never ending greed
Of the naked apes
Who moved out
Of their cave homes
To skyscrapers!

Poem-38

QUEUING FOR 'DARSHAN'[1]

Yin & Yang observe that human beings are in a hurry; to be first everywhere. In the competition driven life, rules of the game are pretty straight - who's first, who's more important, how to manage, manoeuvre, and if need be, manipulate to be first even while queuing for special blessings from the Almighty.

I

We always failed
Not to pay or influence
To those God-keepers
Of the temple!

We want to be first
By hook or by crook
Be in the special group
Exclusively for the VIPs, VVIPs-
Very Important Persons
Very Very Important Persons!

We're lost in manoeuvring
How to manage to be first
At the sanctum sanctorum
Of the temple
Before the idol of the deity
Seeking and negotiating
For fulfillment of desires!

---
[1] Darshan means reaching before the deity of the temple to pray and get blessings!

We don't care no more
Breaking the normal queuing
Of the ordinary poor folks
The poor pilgrims
Who cannot afford to pay
Buying the special blessings from the God!

2

I don't like:
To be in the queue!
But, I know:
I am in the queue!
In the queue;
I don't ever want to be:
In the queue;
I am ordered to be!
In the queue;
For I have no escape!

I know
You are also in the queue!
In the queue;
You don't ever want to be!
In the queue;
You are ordained to be!

We know
 All living and nonliving
Beings and non-beings
Are in the queue!

Queuing for 'Darshan'

The queue;
Nobody ever wants to be!
Against own desire or volition:
As ordained by the laws of Nature!
Time takes its toll:
Unfailingly on time!

3

Even in the Q of the VVIPs
Some breaks all the rules
To reach first
Before the Almighty
To seek boons
To be first ever
Pleading for more wealth, fame, power!

The Goddess of Time
Calls anyone
Mighty or weak
For 'darshan'
Blessing as per her rule!

She is pleased to give
Special blessings early
Out of turn
As per her divine order
Overriding, breaking
All the norms of systematic queuing
Against our wish!

Who can anyway question
The all powerful omniscient
Goddess of Time?
As the queuing
To the final destination is inevitable
I pray the Goddess of Time
To follow the queuing rule for us!
May She permit us
To be in the queue for the full life time
We wish not to be
In the final destination
Not so early
May we pray Thee
Not to summon out of turn
For the ultimate 'Darshan'!

Poem-39

WHISPERING MIND

Yang, narrates his visit to Bodhgaya, the place where Gautam Buddha got enlightenment. He tells his love that the place has induced spirituality in him and he is initiated into a new path in life. He observes that the temple is vibrant with divine atmosphere and he had a self enlightening, mind purifying, experience.

Yang wants Yin to discover the joy of falling in love with the supreme consciousness or power in the world, which according to him, gives pious feelings, humility, true joy and enlightenment.

I

At the Navel of the earth
In Bodhgaya
Under the crimson forehead
Of the evening sky
The Goddess of Dusk
Wore the Sun **bindhi**[1]
Between her bushy dark eyebrows
Formed of dark clouds
Her black curly tresses
Waved in the vales of clouds!
Air was reverberant
With temple bells, cymbals
Sound of conch shells

---
[1] a decorative dot worn in the middle of the forehead, esp by Hindu women

Music and mantras!
Monks prostrated, crawled
And meditated in trance
At **Mahabodhi temple**
With the diamond throne!

Under the foliage
Of the Holy **Mahabodhi tree:**
The great great grandchild
Of the original sacred banyan tree
Under the green leaves
Where the Buddha got enlightened;
I witnessed my Self
In deep meditation!

A sense of awakening
Shook me spellbound
At the place
Where the Buddha concentrated
I worshiped prostrating before Buddha
The great **Karmayogi**[2] of the world
The saint who lived
And died in spreading Dharma[3]!

---

[2] A Real Karma Yogi will perform all his work as a sacrifice for god and will offer the results of his Karma to God. He will not do anything to satiate his personal Ego

[3] one's righteous duty or any virtuous path

2

The prince
Who sacrificed everything
His beloved wife, child
Kingdom, power, comforts
Only to save mankind
From unending sufferings!

'The Four Noble Truths'
Showed the world:
"Life brings sufferings
Unending desires
Caused by cravings
Suffering ends
When one follows the right way!"

Buddha taught
The world the right way
'The Noble Eightfold Path':
"The right understanding
The right resolve, right speech, right action
The right livelihood, right effort
The right awareness, right meditation
To be free
From the Wheel of Life
To attain Nirvana[4]-
The enlightenment!"

---
[4] is the state of being free from suffering (or *dukkha*) insramanic thought

'Nirvana; brings
Right awareness
Cessation of craving
And ignorance'
When we believe
In the Three Jewels:
'The Buddha
Or the perfect wisdom!
The Dharma
Or the law of nature!
The Sangha[5]
Or the monastic practitioners!'

Buddha
The Unique Absolute Refuge
Imperishable, eternal, indestructible!
When the world follows
The five precepts:
'Refrain from taking life
Refrain from committing theft
Refrain from sexual misconduct
Refrain from speaking untruth
Refrain from drugs and alcohol'
Sufferings of living vanish!

3

My mind continued
Whispering to my Soul

---

[5] "association" or "assembly," "company" or "community" with common goal, vision or purpose

The Soul went on
Whispering to my Self
"[6]Om Mani Padme Hum
[7]Om Mani Peme Hung
Behold!
The Jewel in the lotus!"
[8]Om Wagishwari Hum!
[9]Om Vajrapani Hung!
[10]Om Vajraa Sattva Hung!
[11]Om Tare Tuttare Ture Svaha!

I recited Mantra
Of Avalokiteshvara
Mantras of the Buddha
And Buddhist Mother
Inscribed on the Prayer Wheel
On the Mani Wheel
The icon of great compassion!

I rotated the Mani Wheel:
Let my impure body
Turn into pure!
Let my impure speech
Turn into pure!

---

[6] The Buddhist Mantra in Sanskrit.
[7] The Buddhist Mantra in Tibetan form.
[8] This is the Mantra of *Mahaboddhisattva Manjushri*, the Buddha in his wisdom aspect.
[9] The Mantra of the Buddha as protector of the Secret Teachings!
[10] The short Mantra of *Vajrasattva*.
[11] The Mantra of *Jetsun Dolma* or Tara, the mother of the Buddhist.

Let my impure mind
Turn into pure!
Let me be blessed by
Chenrezig[12]!
The Buddha
The embodiment of compassion!

I realize
Life is a journey,
Cycles of births and deaths
Lord
Bestow me with wisdom
Compassion, love and bliss
Transform
The impure body, mind and speech
Into pure exalted body speech
And mind of a Buddha!

---

[12] Embodiment of Compassion in Tibetan Buddhism

Poem-40

THE FIRST RACE OF LIFE

Yang explains the first race of life, which began without the knowledge of the actors in the drama called life. Yang points out that even the selection of the actors who were responsible was under the command of destiny, chance, coincidence or based on the theory of probability. He believes that the actors were in a way said to have been selected by the creator by his own calculations. According to him, the role of destiny seems to be more predominant in the first race of life than pure determinism.

I

The first heartless race of life
Begins the moment
Sperms are ejaculated
Out of the fountain of life
Science speaks
Of the conjugal union of chromosomes
In a live or die choice race of sperms
To unite with an egg
The inevitable struggle
For life leaves only the fittest to survive
Others lose the race
Die in the battlefield dead and forgotten!

Isn't it sheer destiny
That you and I were born
In a particular location on the globe
In a particular moment
In the endless flow of time
As a child
Of a particular male and female
Out of a particular act of love
Or crime, like rape
Or out of one in a series of love games
Played by the actors?

I wouldn't have been me
You wouldn't have been you
He wouldn't have been he
And she wouldn't have been she
Had any other sperm won the race
In fertilizing the lonely available egg
Or merged with some other egg
In another marathon race
Of life played later
Or united in double or triple
To give birth twins....!

2

When many a love game
Ends only in sensual pleasures
When many a torrent of sperms
Annihilates

In hostile environment
When many an egg
Gets flushed out
Without getting
United with a sperm
When many an egg
Gets aborted
Even after fertilization
Isn't it but sheer destiny
That you were born
And you! Not anyone else?

When seeds of life are sown
In fertile land
Under right environment
Some are still decayed or destroyed
A few are only destined to grow
Bringing out
The concealed life in the seed!
The struggle for life
Leaves to live none
But the fittest to survive
The race begins
Without our knowledge
Before our being
Even before we were born!

3

We knew nothing about
The why when

Where what and how of life
The riddle remains
Whether the race of life our choice
Or aren't we mere pawns in the game?

Isn't the race predetermined?
Can science of clones
Change the course of destiny
Keeping everything
Under perfect control!
Isn't it possible
Whether life be created from
Purely non organic substance?

Poem-41

THE BIRD OF GOLD

Yang narrates the life story of a cruel man through this symbolic philosophical fable poem. A butcher wanted to kill his own bird living in him though it happens to be the most valuable bird of gold like the proverbial greedy farmer who had killed the duck who used to lay eggs of gold to have all the eggs in the stomach at a time!

I

Strangulating the bird of gold
Wasn't that easy
Though paralysed, incapacitated
Like a vegetable
And gradually decomposing
On his death bed
The old man was dogged
To take the breath off the bird
After all
He lived his life
All those years
As an experienced butcher
Of the worst species!
Clutching tightly
Those long green legs of the bird

Hanging the bird of gold
Upside down
Pulling, twisting
Squeezing and gyrating
Its long beautiful neck
Plucking its plumage
of purple, violet, blue, green and pink
Pulling gold tails, crowned over
Red rubies and diamonds:
Many a time

The old man
Continued his struggle
Dogged to kill the bird mercilessly
Like The greedy legendary fool in the fable
Who had killed the bird
Who used to lay eggs of gold:
The old butcher in the old man
Brutally attacked the bird
To maim, injure and wound it seriously
To incapacitate the bird
If not possible to kill
To stop it from flying away
Out of him leaving him forever!

2

"I won't let you go
The Bird of Gold
I've brought you up
All these years

The Bird of Gold

Given you food to eat
Drinks to quench your thirst
You're the bird
Who lives in me
Makes me sleep
Pecks me in the morning
Waking me up!

If you try to leave me
Alone again
Sure I'll strip off
Your feathers of gold
One by one
Pull out sure
All those ethereal beautiful flowers
On the head
Pluck out your eyes
Of diamonds
And make you blind
Puncture your heart
To bleed to death
And tear off your body apart
In many a piece
Spilling your blue blood
On the earth
You know my bird
Haven't I been a master butcher in life?"

3

It was a new moon day
Darkness descended
Into his room
Clouds cried aloud
Thunder banged
Quacked the earth
Wind roared in fury
And it rained endlessly!

The old man was laid alone
On his death bed
Abandoned
In a dark stinking dungeon of a room
Even a beam of light
Given birth by a loud thunder
Feared to tread in his room
And died in a moment
Failing to bring
Even a flicker of hope
In his doomed life!

The Bird of Gold was determined:
"You're an old, tattered, aged
Worn out and stinking rag of mine!
I'll abandon
This outdated apparel of yours
I hate to wear it any longer
This decadent garment of yours

I 'm getting new clothes
Tonight itself!"

"Leave me not!
Please reject me not
My Bird of Gold!
You're my life
You're my soul!
You're my self
You're my spirit!
I'm nothing without you
You've been perching in me
Since my birth
I have no one
But you!"
Cried the old man
In agony and pain!

4

His sunk yellow eyes
Caved deep in his hollow cheeks
Formed two deep pools of tears!
He knew
The Bird of Gold is immortal
Invisible
Invincible and indestructible
Omnipresent, omniscient, omnipotent!
In vain
Were the efforts of the butcher
To kill the bird!

Reminiscent of
Jesus after the crucifixion
Rejuvenated the bird
From the torture
Sang the song of liberation
Flapping its wings of gold feathers
Bejewelled with diamond crown
In absolute darkness of midnight
The old man heard its whistling call
Reminiscent of **Panchajanyam**[1] of **Lord Krishna**

He witnessed helplessly
The Bird of Gold was flying off
Out of him forever
Abandoning his rotten rib cage
The nest which had the heart clock
Once continued ticking inside!

5

The pumping machine
Stopped inside the chamber
The ventilator failed
To hold breath any longer
He heard the song
Of the eternal bird clearly:
"Let me leave right now
Nobody can stop me any longer
You're the dirty torn outdated garment
I want to wear my new dress right now!"

---
[1] the divine conch of Vishnu

"Vasamsi jirnani yatha vihaya[2]
Navani grhnati naro parani
Tatha sarirani vihaya jirnana
Nanyani samyati navani dehi"

The Bird of Gold flew away
To penetrate into another womb
To get into another embryo
To enliven another living being
To wear a new apparel
To perch on a new nest!

The old man's mouth
Fiercely split open
Tongue lashed for a while
And stopped
Eyes opened wide
And remained still staring
The Bird of Gold left
The old body cage forever!

---

[2] As a person gives up old and worn out garments and accepts new apparel, similarly the embodied soul giving up old and worn out bodies verily accepts new bodies.

Poem-42

JOURNEY OF A SOUL

Yang is philosophical these days as he has more time to ponder over metaphysical and ontological thoughts. Being religious and enjoying reading spiritual and philosophical books, he shares his thoughts and what he understands from each life experience with Yin. He touches upon the philosophy of life enshrined in the cycles of life and birth or the Wheel of Life as explained in the Buddhist theology.

1

In cycles of births and deaths
In rotation of the Wheel of Life
In a never ending journey of souls
A soul entered into my body
Taking me for another Stream of Life!

By volition or imposition of the Almighty
The soul got incarcerated in the cage
The mortal body encapsulated the immortal soul
Heartbeats of the clock of life started ticking!

2

The apparels the souls wear are varied
Some are colorful, fashionable, and beautiful
But many a soul gets in the race imperfect attire
Of subhuman size, defectively, awful, ragged

Men in their folly quarrel over the color of their dress—
Black! White! Brown! Yellow! Hispanic! Asian!
When the candle of life extinguishes
Cage crumbles, soul gets out of the prison
Flies away soul like an invisible, immortal bird of gold
Fluttering and flapping its wings
Keeping neck stretched towards heaven above!
Matters the least the dejected apparel is buried or burnt
Or allowed to be consumed by vultures

Balance sheet of the deeds of the mortal man
Is prepared, balancing assets and liabilities
Calculating negative and positive balances
Accounting for all good and bad deeds
By those who know the departed soul!

3

Let me listen to the chronicle of my soul
The autobiographical saga of its journey
Amidst the ticking time machine called heart
I wonder in awe, thinking of the mission of my life!

Buddha taught "The Wheel of Life
Rotates with its six spokes
Pushed by ignorance, desires, sensual cravings
Life cycle changes continuously over the six realms
From the world of **Devas**[1], **Asuras**[2], humans
To the world of animals, **Pretas**[3] and hell!"

---
[1] deities
[2] power-seeking deities, sometimes referred to as demons or sinful
[3] Ghosts

Oh! Lord!
The cycles of births and deaths are painful
How to stop the Wheel of Life!
How to attain **Nirvana**?
Before the bubbling water of life fall on rocks
Or dry up in barren thirsty sands of desert!

Let me look above in salutation of the Maker
Praying for mercy and love, in folded hands
Seeking apology, for selfish wrangles and quarrels
Purifying my thoughts, words, and action in Thy name!

Poem-43

RIVER OF LIFE

Yin and Yang are energy vibes flowing in the universe, have been conspicuous in nature, evident in living things in varied formats, styles and forms, though the human animal contradicts, challenges and disbelieves these fundamental truths in his limited exposure to science. Human animal learns and relearns and de-learns to understand the mysteries in nature.

Yang reminisces his life journey with Yin and their experience of hiking along the panoramic Himalayan terrains, and traversing along the route of the River Indus and her mate River Zanskar uniting at Nimu valley and flowing beyond till the river joins the ocean and even beyond following the full cycle!

I

Out of the womb
Of the glaciers
Sprang forth the stream
Flowed down
Pure crystal clear water!

Criss-crossing
The crevices
Forests, mountains, deep ravines
Vales, cascades of Mother Nature!

We hiked
On the mountains
Enjoying meadows of green
Vales of flowers and herbs!

Crossing rocky terrains
Along the high altitude deserts
Traversing dangerously risky tracks
Where only stones bloomed!

Over slippery, curvaceous
Bare hips of hills
In the heat dust
Inclement weather!

We climbed
Up and down
Exploring virgin territories
Witnessing nude burnt
Skeleton hill groins:

Proof of endless rapes
Of the Mother Nature
By the greedy men
On the Planet Earth!
Depressed were we
Not able to rescue
Our Mother!

2

In the sanctum sanctorum
Of the Mother Nature
In front of the mighty home
Of ice glacier peaks
In the exploited
Raped and gradually dying
Rapidly aging red
Sun tanned environ:

We saw;
A tiny little child of a river
Growing big, and bigger;
Becoming:
Blue Indus River
At Leh!

Indus travelled with us
Along the undulating high altitude
Ancient caravan routes
Creating heavenly oases!

Of exotic green vales, all along
Giving life giving
Pure crystal clear water
From the glaciers
To the multihued arid
Desert mountain wilderness!

Soft is the way of the water
Melting winning over hard rock!
It's the loving way of the feminine
Giving way to win over the heart
Of even the strongest of men!

Dotting with **gompas**
The temples of the Buddhists
Clutching on the underbellies
Of craggy hilltops
With **chortens**[1]
Prayer wheels, prayer flags
Fluttering all over!

3

The river flows
Fast down the hills
Roaring, laughing
Giggling, screaming
At times!

Meeting
Intersecting
Departing in the course!

Indus found her mate
Muddy brown
Zanskar
At Nimu valley!

---
[1] dharma place/seat

We witnessed
Both getting lost
In each other's charm
Hugging and loving!
Merging and uniting
Bubbling in exuberance
In orgasmic effervescence
In bliss mating
To be one and being one!

The mighty great Indus
Flowed further down
After the confluence
Losing individual identity!

4

In the flow, getting slow
She gets enervated
Polluted, senile:

The river joined the sea
At the end of its course:
Merging into waves
Urging to be clouds again;
And pouring down in rain!

She prays to be reborn again!
As tiny baby stream
Somewhere In the womb:
Of the glacier mountains
In the cycle of the flow!

Like the River of Life
Flowing all along
Merging into the infinite
Ocean of Consciousness!

5

In sublime bliss
Babe, we knew
We were trekking
The mountain
Of life together
Flowing like
River of life
To its destination!

We prayed:
"May He enlighten our minds
And lead the way of life to ultimate joy
The Supreme Bliss, infinite ecstasy!"

"Sarvesham Svastirbhavatu
Sarvesham Shantirbhavatu
Servesham Poornam Bhavatu
Sarvesham Mangalam Bhavatu!"

Poem-44

ETERNAL ENERGY FLOW

Yin and Yang have been circumambulating the world in the speed of mind waves in number of times as they please to observe, oversee, understand and watch life on earth and the living since the days of Big Bang or even before. They know the presence of the supreme consciousness. Yang wants to make it clear to the human being that there is Supreme Power of Nature, call it whatever way. According to Yang despite having been experimenting with life the human being takes so much time to understand even a little bit of mystery of the world. He feels that what the man knows by now may be only a fraction of the secrets and many of the things human beings believe may even prove to be not factually correct in years to come.

I

Lord you are there everywhere
For those who believe in you!
Proving that you exist or not
May be an atheist's pastime!

In the bloated ego of ignorance
Man first thought the Sun
Revolved round flat plane earth
A non elliptical non globular earth
Punished the man who told the truth!
In the lives of the blatant egotistic

Ignorant, nincompoop
The stone-man
Thought he knew too much!

Killed animals left and right
Ate raw flesh like animals
Walked naked like animals
He knew not he was naked!

He knew not fire and wheel existed
He knew not later innovations
He was blind to see anything
Even his own nudity!

2

Existed everything in the air
Even from the very beginning
Electrons, protons, neutrons
Electricity, electromagnetic waves,
Omnipotent technology
Omniscient Internet!
Omnipresent electromagnetism!
As manifestations
Of the supreme power of knowledge!

The 'Web of life' is now the reality
Interconnected brains interact
Internationally connected, networked
Engaging the hearts and minds
Exchanging thoughts, emotions, ideas!

Human beings are hooked in millions
All pooh-poohed by the earlier men!
Proving that electrons could be there
Test tube baby could be made cloned
As incredible, blasphemy, non-existed!

3

Experiencing you in every moment
Is my mission and passion in life!
When minds are tuned well
In the right frequency
Messages are transmitted
Broadcast and telecast
In streams, vibes and in mental waves!

We experience that telepathy works
We know radio electronic waves Internet
All wonders of nature
That we discovered existed
Whether we could discover earlier or not
Fire, light, electricity
Radiations, magnetism, World Wide Web
All were there in nature even before we captured!

Right before me
My atheist friend challenged my Guru[1]
"You God man!
Prove your God exists!"

---
[1] one who is regarded as having great knowledge, wisdom and authority in a certain area, and who uses it to guide others (teacher)

My Guru was ice cool; smiled and asked:
"Have you seen air, while breathing?
Have you seen, my friend,
Your mind while challenging me?

You know, dear, scientists prove life is matter
Atoms, chemicals and what not
If so, why can't we make life
Out of chemicals, atoms, matter and what not
Without taking any organic cells from the living?"

4

My Master! I've no questions
Nor do have I doubts
I believe in telepathy
Like electromagnetic waves
Encircles earth, space, outer world
In the velocity faster than light
In the velocity of mind in mental waves
In the endless Ocean of Consciousness
Sending and receiving mental waves!

Lord, bless me!
Let me pilot my small vessel safely
In the turbulent currents of life
Let me close my eyes for a while
Let me ignore those uninvited thoughts
Let me focus on my sixth chakra
On my forehead right between the eyebrows
Let me experience the divine illumination within me!

5

Oh my Creator, let me purify my mind
In transcendental meditation!
Let me experience the ethereal bliss in me
Let me hear the divine voice of yours in me

Let me feel your presence in every breath of mine
Let me fill you in my Mind, Soul, Spirit and Self
Let time, space, distance, media, all obstructions
And impediments vanish between you and me
Let all unwarranted distinctions vaporise in thin air!

Let me delve deep into the spiritual ocean of eternity
Let my body, mind, intellect, soul, self be in fusion

May the wavelengths of thoughts, emotions, feelings
Get tuned into the right frequency
May the eternal divine energy flow through my spine
May it unite me
With the Supreme Energy flow of the Universe!

Poem-45

YOU GIFTED THE SUN ITS ENERGY

According to Yang, there is no controversy about the existence of some sort of supreme consciousness, call it God, Nature, Energy Flow of the Universe. He has no quarrel over these fundamental issues though he finds that man is always in a hurry to establish nothing exists without proof. The problem, according to Yang, is that even to prove properly one may need to be capable of understanding and using the appropriate methodology. Yang talks about the omnipresence of the Supreme Being in the Universe.

I

Oh my Lord
You gifted the Sun its energy!
Lightening
Thundering sound and luminosity!
The moon
Its smiling glow, stars their twinkling!

You gifted Fire heat
 Air its velocity and power
You gifted Water to rivers, lakes, and ocean
And waves to water!
You gifted Space the ether

Ether, infinite expanse of sky!
You gifted Earth to life
Life
Heartbeats, growth and decay!

You are the Master of my Soul, my Self
I am part of Thee
The ultimate consciousness—
The supreme bliss!

2

Lord
Leaves bristle in the air
Bringing your footsteps
Flowers bloom in the garden
Carrying the scent you wear!

Birds sing your songs
Rivers compose your music
Sound of life reverberates in air, water, earth
I feel your presence everywhere!

Sky is filled by you
Earth is filled by you
Your presence is felt by all
Animate and inanimate!

You put heart in me
And I put you in my heart!
You are in me
I am in you!

And you are everywhere!
Why am I searching you
Here, there and everywhere?

3

Bestow me
My Lord your blessings
Let me be
Part of the life that grows!

Let me be
Part of the fire that blazes!
Let me be
Part of the wind that blows!

Let me be
Part of the energy that spreads!
Let me be
Part of the light that illuminates!

Let me be
Part of the earth that gives life!
Let me be
Part of the water-the elixir of life!

Let me form part of the ether
That expands infinitely!
Let me, my Lord
Be part of thee
The infinite energy flow!

Poem-46

TAMING THE MONKEY

Yang has been initiated into some sort of spiritualism these days in the absence of Yin. Having too much time in life to ponder and understand the subtle truths, he spends time in self discovery by reading religion, philosophy, metaphysics, ontology and subjects like that. He tries to follow Vivekananda principles in life. He wants to tame his monkey mind and does the best possible methods to do so. Yang knows that mind is the source of happiness and cause of worries. As he understands, the prime objective of life is to reduce sorrows and increase the joy of living. Once the mind is trained and tamed, he can feel quite healthy psychologically, as enhanced mental health brings increased physical health and happiness.

The heart went on ticking
Body clock failed not to record life!
The pulse continued pounding
Lungs inhaled and exhaled
Blood flowed with Oxygen
Giving life giving energy to cells!

The monkey mind cared little
Indulged in its relentless pranks
The eternal quest went on:
"Lord!

Who am I? –
The body!
Mind!
Soul!
 Self!
Or Atman[1]?"

The monkey was fully drunk
With the wine of endless desires
Stung by the scorpion of jealousy
Possessed by ego, anger, hatred
Overpowered by lust, desire and greed
The monkey continued
Its acrobatics on mind tree!

Unable to control
The mischievous ape
I posed a few questions to my Guru:
"How do I discipline the wild beast?
How do I stop him swinging left to right?
How do I stop it playing negative games?
My Master!
How do I overpower negative thoughts?"

My Guru advised
"Witness your mind monkey for a while
Understand the games the monkey plays
Be cool! Be calm!
Be patient! Be strong willed!

---

[1] is a philosophical term used within Hinduism and Vedanta to identify the soul whether in global sense (world's soul) or in individual sense (of a person own soul)

Taming the Monkey

Please do capture your wild monkey
Have absolute control of its movements
Get ready!
Train the mischievous ape
Right now!"

I was at sea
Knowing not how to start
Guru told: "Sit in **Padmasana**[2]!
Purify your body
And cleanse of the mind
Meditation and Mantras may help
Start **Pranayam**[3] and **Meditation**!"

My master helped me to initiate:
"Control breathing in and out
Inhale Oxygen with good thoughts
Exhale bad air along with toxins, ill feelings!
Hold the breath for a while
Relax and energise your body!"

My trainer knew what he was doing:
"Put the monkey mind in to your heart
Let there be a lotus in your heart
Let there be light, effulgent flame in your heart
Let your monkey mind be there at any centre
Any energy centres along the spine

---
[2] a cross-legged sitting posture originating in meditative practices of ancient India, in which the feet are placed on the opposing thighs
[3] a method of controlling prana or life force through the regulation of breathing

At the third eye between the eyebrows
Or put your monkey mind in the brain
Let there be a lotus let there be a flame
Let there be sound of bells chiming at a distance
Let there be constant drumming in the ear drum
Let there be specks of light becoming bigger and bigger!

Like an oyster look for the special star shines in the sky
The oyster knows then it will rain
The oyster comes then to the surface
To absorb a drop of rain falling from the sky
Into its shell and dives down into the bottom of the sea
To meditate patiently to make a pearl out of the drop!

When mind is tuned in perfect harmony
A pin dropping down makes a thunder
Take up one idea
Make that idea your life
Think of it, dream of it
Live on that idea
That idea is yours
That idea is you
Let the mind, brain, soul
Body, muscles, nerves
Every part of your body
Every organ, every cell
Be filled with that idea
Be full of that idea
Enthralled, enchanted by the idea

And just leave every other idea alone!
That's is the key to success!

Run away from negative vibes
Persons, places, disturbing evil forces
Evil Ideas, distracting thoughts and people
Let you be determined:
Swear; "I will drink the ocean!"
And "at my will mountain will crumble up"
Have that idea, will, energy
Work hard you will reach your goal!,"

"Let your mind travel the path of the breaths
Invite not any thoughts, ignore them!

If still bother you know the thoughts
Count them, name them and label them!
Let the horizon of your mind be empty
Like the infinite expanse of the sky and space!
Feel warmth inside!
Enjoy the energy flow within!"

My teacher was determined to help me:
"When you're ready for Meditation
Close the eyes
Concentrate on the mind
Focus between the eyebrows
Try to see a divine light flickering!

Continue practising meditation
Be aware of the Seven Chakras

Try effortlessly to align the chakras
From the base of the spine to the crown!

Elevate your **Prana**[4] gradually to the crown
Let the **Kundalini** in you awaken!
Tame the mischievous monkey mind
Enjoy peace, happiness, and bliss infinite!"

Like a baby
Laying close to the bosom of her mother
I laid in **Shavasana**[5]
Close to the bosom of Mother Earth

I began differentiating the flow of thoughts
Knowing the thoughts good and bad
Counting the thoughts
Naming and labelling
And continued the meditation
To tame the monkey mind!

>Om! May all be happy!
>May all be healthy!
>May we all experience what is good!
>And let no one suffer!

>"Sarve Bhavantu Sukhinah!
>Sarve Santu Niramayah!
>Sarve Bhadrani Pasyantu!
>Ma Kascit Dukha Bhagbhavet!"

---
[4] a vital, life-sustaining force of living beings and vital energy
[5] a relaxing posture intended to rejuvenate body, mind and spirit

Poem-47

CLEANSING OF THE MIND

After working on taming and training the wild monkey called mind, Yang endeavours in cleansing of the polluted mind. Mind filled with negative vibes and puerile thoughts spoil good life and joy of living. He finds that environment both internal and external influences human mind. Yang notices that when accumulated things pile up at home over the years, it impacts adversely on the mind. The carried over relationship problems cause pain and depression. Yang therefore wants to get out of dirty environs at home and cleanse his mind from the accumulated unwarranted experiences to bring life back on its track.

I

Sweet home becomes
A dumping yard
Heaps of rubbish
Scatter all around:

Faded clothes
Dilapidated old furniture
Dusty artefacts
Abandoned utensils, e-waste...

Germinate toxic
Worms, germs, virus

Bacteria, fungi
And micro-organisms:
All stare at me
As mementos of life gone by!

2

In the bottom
Of the subconscious mind
Helplessly caught
In one's own cobwebs:
Amidst the ever procreating
Own created mess:

Mind swings
In a trapezium
From one to the other!

Left over, dejected
Lost use of ideas
Broken, torn, ravaged
Bleeding, wounded
Despondent, rejected
Feelings and emotions!

All sorts of baggage
Carried over the years
Creates new breeding grounds
For psychic disorders!

Senses start galloping
Amuck like wild horses

Cleansing of the Mind

In the horizon of the mind uncontrolled
The chariot of desires
Get dragged away hither thither
The rein gets strained
Sandstorms are everywhere!

3

The charioteer sits
As helpless witness
There is no **Krishna** to guide **Arjun**[1]
Having lost all powers of control!

A bloodied **Kurukshetra**[2] like war is on
Between the good and evil forces
Between positive and negative energy!

Let me clean my home
Let me throw away the garbage

Let the mind
Be awash of the toxic emotions
Let a few lamps light up
In the temple of my mind!

Let flowers and scents
Decorate and bring fragrance

---

[1] *Arjuna* or *Arjun* is one of the Pandavas, the heroes of the Hindu epic *Mahâbhârata*. *Arjuna*, whose name means 'bright', 'shining', 'white' or 'silver', was such a peerless archer that he is often referred to as Jishnu the undefeatable

[2] a dynastic struggle between sibling clans of *Kauravas* and the *Pandavas* for the throne of *Hastinapura* resulted in a battle in which a number of ancient kingdoms participated as allies of the rival clans. The location of the battle was *Kurukshetra* in the modern state of Haryana in India

Let the green leaves of life bloom
Let my mind
Be inundated
By sublime love
Purity of thought
Benevolence and compassion!

4

Oh, Lord!
Lead me from untidiness to tidiness
Sickness to health
Sorrows to happiness
Darkness to light
Ignorance to knowledge
Unawareness to awareness
Melancholy to bliss!

Lord! Lead me from
Unawareness to awareness
From darkness to light
From death to immortality
Let peace be there!

"Om Asato Maa Sadgamaya
Tamaso Maa Jyotirgamaya
Mrityormaa Amritamgamaya
Om Shantih! Shantih! Shantih!"

Poem-48

MAYA CALLED LIFE

Yang joins an Ashram and seeks the help of a Guru in unravelling the mysteries and secrets of the journey called life. In the drama of life, he observes that, when confronted with the fundamental questions of life Who am I?, Why am I here? What is the purpose of life? Why is it happening to me? Why am I like this? Where am I going? Is there a life after death? Etc. answer lies in religion, philosophy and metaphysics.

Yang tells Yin about the Maya concept of Hindu mythology and explains to her how human beings start the journey of life even before realising that they are in it. He finds that people had no control on the event of birth or the actors responsible for that act. They are simply made aware of the destination. What one can do is only trying to influence the course of the journey by identifying the inner strength and deriving the maximum power by networking with the Universal energy flow.

I

Life is **Maya**[1]
An illusion; said
Vedas and Vedanta!

Life is series of dreams
Good dreams and nightmares!

---
[1] the principal concept which manifests, perpetuates and governs the illusion and dream of duality in the phenomenal Universe

Life is a journey
We had started even before
We realised that we were in it!

We had no control about the beginning
Path we feel we are choosing
Destination we are made to know

We know we have no escape
But we know not
When and how we reach!

Life is a drama
Says Shakespeare
Play well; act well
Till your role is done
You are allowed to play!

Disillusioned I sit
In the dark corners of my life
Fused were only those brain cells
Carrying good messages and thoughts!
Surprisingly active cells carried
Negative feelings like poison!
How do I remember only good things?
How do I delete bad memories from brain?
How do I live happy in the present?

2

Meeting my guru changed
The course of my life thereafter

Maya called Life

My master made me realize
This life is an illusion of the mind
A dream for reality
Like seeing snake in rope!

Like having a nightmare
Of fire engulfing your home
You wake up in between
Witnessing real fire swallowing you!

Like ejaculating in dreams
While conjugating the beloved
Getting up realizing
No female around
Witnessing only the clothes
Stained by the generative fluid!

Like in quantum physics
And the theory of relativity
Talk about time travel
Visiting our great grandfather
By travelling backwards in time!

3

My teacher explained:
"Mind is the knot that joins
Consciousness and matter
Pierce the veil to glimpse
The transcendent truth!"

Guru made it clear:
"Reflection of Brahman[2]
The supreme god
Falls on Maya
The enchantress divine!
Duality of real and truth
Played like a magic
Only magician Brahman knew
It's pure magic, not real!"

I gave him my ears
He taught me how
Lord **Krishna** enlightened **Arjuna:**
"I am the womb of all things
Source and dissolution of the universe
My womb is the Mother Nature
In that I place the seed
Embryo of life!
A being is born from the union
Of the knower and the field
The union of **Purusha** and **Prakriti**
Or **Shiva** and **Shakti**
Or Spirit and Matter!"

4

My teacher enlightened me:
"In the deceit of Maya
Life creates a false dichotomy
Between self and the universe

---

[2] priest

Maya called Life

A duality between mind and body
Brahman and self
Supreme self and the pure consciousness
Self and 'I' consciousness
And consciousness and physical matter!"

My master narrated that
The Sikhs went to their guru
Pleading Oh! Baba!
Maya cheats us!
Guru Granth Sahib[3] reminded:
"Men are attached to Maya
Men forget their Father
The Maker of the World!

This body is the puppet of Maya
Men do selfless service and sacrifice
Prayers, meditation, congregation
Good deeds for penance!"

5

My guru narrated the Zen Master story
'I put a goose in a bottle
The bottle whose neck is narrow
The goose grows big
I want the goose to be out!'

I told: 'Break the bottle and get the goose out'
'No! The bottle is precious not to be broken!'
'Let the goose be dead in that case'; I pleaded:

---
[3] is the holy scripture and the final Guru of the Sikhs

'That goose is you, just take the goose out!'
'If I'm the goose, life is precious
And my life is the most precious for me!
Let the bottle be broken, life be saved!'

My guru laughed:
'First of all you were never in the bottle!
Simply watch, be an observer, be in and watch
You're out and the feeling that you're in
It is illusion – Maya!'

6

I chose the golden path
Purified my body
Cleansed of my mind
I felt like a new man
Coming out of ashes of ignorance
Like mythical phoenix bird!

Owning something or not
Now matters me the least
Matters me is the feeling
Of owning everything but nothing!
Walking along the park I feel
I own the park and the sky above
I try to see me reflected in everyone
I feel that the Maker and I own the world!

What will I do even if I own the world?
Just be around witnessing and experiencing?

I want to take away the 'I' from me
Proud to be him vicariously
Who makes a difference in life
Makes the world a better place to live!

7

Guru you made me realize
Futility of ego, desire and possession
You taught me to live being human
Join hands with goodness and be content!

From the very beginning in the macrocosm
I remained ignorant of my existence
Later when I knew I existed
I could figure out nothing of me
I knew something of me in this journey
In relation to things, beings and objects
I am aware now I exist but to be detached yet
Not bound by limitless ego and unending desires!

8

Let me accelerate my journey
Towards the destination
To be liberated completely
To be detached, satisfied entirely
In an ultimate state of awareness

Pleased with
The sublime bliss
Content fully
Fulfilled eventually

Into a state
Of absolute awareness!

Where I know
I am the existence
I exist and I am I
Aham Brahmasmi[4]!

---
[4] I am Brahman

Poem-49

THE AWAKENING

Yang after serious meditation and adopting positive vibes in living, starts experiencing bit by bit an experience of knowing things more clearly. He understands the frivolousness of arrogance, showing off, aggression and not being helpful, kind, concerned and connected with others and being self centred with always an axe to grind in everything for oneself. Yang narrates to his life partner how he has been made to know the purpose of life by great religious teachers. He narrates the Tantric concept of being aware of the inner strength and energy that helps self realization and self actualization. Yang believes that awakening of the inner energy is the first step to empower oneself and join with the positive energy vibes in the universe to make a difference in the life of the hapless in the world.

I

I've come to know now
In the twilight of my life
My own serpent
The dormant snake in me
Sleeps lazy:
Coiled down un-awakened
At the base of my spine
At **Muladhara**
The root receptacle!

How do I wake you up?
Prana;
The inner energy in me!
Why do you sleep?
My serpent, my energy
Wasn't I born with you?

2

I sat in Padmasana;
In the Yoga posture
I was comfortable in meditation
Closing my eyes
Witnessing flickering bright spark
Illumination before the sixth eye
The divine brilliant golden glow
Between the eyebrows
Right at the centre of the forehead!

3

My Guru came to my rescue:
"Perform **rajayoga**[1]!
Meditate, concentrate, focus!
By the power of meditation
May **Sushmna**
The central spinal chord open!
May **Prana** be awakened!
Let your mind transmit energy like waves
Let the divine energy flow through you!"

---

[1] concerned principally with the cultivation of the mind using meditation *(dhyana)* to further one's acquaintance with reality and finally achieve liberation

My master was serious in what he said:
"May the awakened serpent travel upwards
From chakra to chakra from lotus to lotus
From **Muladhara** to **Sahasrara:**
From the last bone in the spinal chord
To ovaries/prostate to navel
To heart to throat to pineal gland
To top of the head
From the Pelvic plexus
To the crown of the head!

    4

May **Ojas** –
The energy latent and unused
Travel through
The central canal of the spinal chord
Bringing energy
To every nerve every cell!"

My tutor continued the session:
 "Continue meditation
Be a **Rajayogi**[2]!
Till the thousand petalled lotus
On your head at Sahasrara –
The crown chakra - blossoms!

Till you liberate from the bondage of life
From this vale of sorrows and pain
From the chains

---
[1] One who practices Rajyoga

Of limitless desires and sorrows
To merge into Thee
The Supreme Consciousness
The ultimate energy flow in the universe!"

5

Having felt absolute vacuum in the mind
Absorbed deep in an inner voice
Overpowered by the divine music
Reverberating chanting of Mantras
I felt a celestial vibration
Intense unexplainable
Celestial sensation!

Alternating warm
And cold ethereal feeling
Started crawling my Kundalini
Like a serpent
From the base of my spine
Muladhara
Aiming toward Sahasrara!

My Master recited
The **Mrityunjaya Mantra:**
"Oh Lord!
You hold in your three eyes
The Sun, the Moon, and the Fire
Master of all masters
Master of all senses and qualities
Let me bow down to you!"

"Om Triyambakam Yajamahe
Sugandhim Pushtivardhanam
Urvarukamiva Bandhanan
Mrityor Mukheeya Maamritat!"

6

My teacher asked me
To pray to the Goddess then:
"Oh! Divine Mother!
I bow to thee!

I surrender before you
Devi **Tripurasundarai**
Embodiment of all mothers
Shri, Saraswati, Parvati, united in one!

Oh! Mother of all mothers
Embodiment of the supreme knowledge
Embodiment of the ultimate wealth
Embodiment of chastity and goodness

Mother of the supreme energy flow
Embodiment of limitless energy
The infinite bliss, I bow to Thee
The omnipotent, omnipresent power house!

Poem-50

CHURNING THE MIND LAKE

Yang in the incarnation of Darling, wants Yin or Babe to join him to the most important pilgrimage to Manasa Sarovar in Tibet. He believes that life can be relived in purity by adopting subtle principles and good feelings for everyone. He advocates purification of body, mind and soul in the backdrop of pilgrimage to Mount Kailash[1] and Manasa Sarovar[2]!

I

Babe
If you believe
If our legs can carry our body
If our mind can withstand
The churning of good and bad:

Like the legendary churning
Of the Milk Ocean by Gods and demons
To find 'Amrita'
The nectar
Which makes immortality:
If we can enjoy

---

[1] A Himalayan peak regarded as abode of Hindu god, Shiva
[2] A fresh-water lake in Tibet.

The soul purifying
Ascend
Descend
And circumambulation:

If our heartbeats
Pulse rates, breathings
Can harmonise:

My request, Honey
Let us go
To Manasa Sarovar!
The lake of the mind
Created by Brahma
The maker of this world!

2

Let us be there
At the holy crystal clear
Glacier Peak!

The precious jewel
Of the snows,
The water peak;
The womb of the four rivers!

Flowing in four directions,
Dividing the valleys,
Mountains;
In four regions!
Let us be there

At Mount Kailash!
Let us witness
The origin of the Sutlej[3]
Flowing to the West!

Let us enjoy
The beginning of the Indus
Flowing to the North!
Let us see
The birth of the Karnali[4]
Daughter of the Ganges
Flowing to the South!

3

Let us dip ourselves
In the infant
Virgin Brahmaputra
Flowing to the East!

Let us cleanse of our body
Mind, self, spirit, and soul
Let us purify our body
Mind, self, spirit, and soul
Let us forget
All that went wrong in life
Let us feel the touch
Of the Almighty
Deep inside

---
[3] A river in the Himalayan mountain range
[4] Tributary of river Ganges

Let us listen
To his whispering
From the core
Of our soul!

4

You know, Babe
We cannot stop:
The legs
Of the time machine
Walking!

Nobody even
The Almighty
Can stop
Time
From moving
Even for a moment!

Believe me or not
Nobody had
A perfect life
Perhaps
Even the Gods

Buddha, Mahavira
 Zoroaster, Krishna
Jesus or the Prophet!
So why do we
Feel guilty of the past?
No chance to relive

The past life!
Only are corrections
Possible for the future
Nobody ever lived felt
Everything happened
Was great!

Mistakes, omissions
And commissions
Are part of living!

5

We don't know
Nobody knows so far
Whether there is
Life after this!

Or are we going
To hell or heaven
Or are we going
To float like white clouds
Or move like waves, air
To be space or ether?
Nobody so far can say
Whether we take birth
As insect, creature, animal
Plant or human being!
So why worry
Let us forget

All that went wrong in life
All that we could not change
In the course of the journey!

6

Let us forget us
 And let us forgive us
Let us dissolve the ego
In the lake of Manasa Sarovar
The lake of the mind
Created by the Creator!

Let us eliminate
All bad feelings
Bad thoughts
Bad words, bad actions!

Let us dip our body
Mind, self, spirit, soul
In the holy water!

Let us wash off all sins
In the holy womb
Of the four rivers
The sublime crystal pure
Glacier water
Of the river peak!

7

Let us have a rebirth
After the holy dip
Let us be humane
Kind, caring, and gracious!
Let our heart, mind, self
Spirit, soul be inundated
By pure, sublime, compassion
Benevolence and love!

If possible let us go
To Jerusalem
 Mecca
Medina
Lumbini

And all the religious places
In the world
To take a rebirth in this life itself
Being human
Out of the ashes
Like the Phoenix bird!

"Aum... Aum...Aum...
Sahana Vavatu Sahanou Bhunaktu
Sahaveeryam Karavava Hi
Tejasvina Vadhitamastu
Mavidh Visha Vahava Hi
Aum Shanti ...Shanti...Shanti..."

Oh Lord!
Let us be together, Let us eat together!
Let us produce the energy together!
Let there be no limit to our energies!
Let there be no ill feelings among us!
Oh Lord! Let there be peace, peace, peace!

Poem-51

THE BLACK MOTHER GODDESS OF TIME

Yang tells the story of Kali, the Black Mother Goddess of Time to Yin. He explains to her that the mystery of creation of the cosmos and the living is linked with the primordial mother goddess of time, which is the cosmic womb in the universe. Yang makes Yin to recollect how she was all alone in the very beginning sailing across the cosmic waters.

I

Babe
Let me tell you the story of
Our Divine Black Primordial God Mother?

In the very beginning
When there was nothing
But infinite bottomless abyss
Our Eternal Mother-'Ammavaru'[1]
Sailed in absolute darkness on a lotus boat
Over the cosmic water and one day
She laid three eggs secretly on the lotus leaf!

Emerged out of the egg
The Divine Gods

---

[1] according to a minor Hindu belief, is an ancient goddess who laid the egg that hatched Brahma, Shiva and Vishnu

Brahma! Vishnu! Shiva!
Like God Father! God Son! And The Holy Ghost
In the Cosmic Womb Mandala[2]!

Afire with irrepressible desire and passion
Pleaded our Ammavaru to gods:
"Come on! Gods! Let us marry, enjoy, mate
Procreate life in the universe!"

The Gods refused
Furious was Ammavaru
Blazing with fire in her third eye
Located between her eyebrows
In the middle of her forehead!

Gods got scared:
"Ok! We'ill marry you; Ammavaru!
Gift your third eye to us!"

Burning with lust, Ammavaru plucked
Her third eye, gave to Shiva!
Amma lost all her divine powers
Her skin wrinkled, body shrunk, dried up
And withered, hair turned grey!

Brahma, Vishnu and Shiva
Created earth
Out of her body and ruled over!

---

[2] is a concentric diagram having spiritual and ritual significance in both Buddhism and Hinduism

2

"Darling
Won't you tell me
The story of our Black Mother Goddess Kali
The omnipresent, omniscient, omnipotent
All destroying goddess of time!

Why is she wearing an apron of human hands
And a garland of human heads:
Holding freshly chopped human head
And the murder weapon dripping with blood?

Why is the goddess of power standing
On the white body of her consort Shiva
With her luxuriant hair, completely dishevelled
Face red in fury, tongue protruding?"

3

"Babe, you know
She is the energy responsible
For the dissolution of the universe
She shows 'abhaya mudra'[3] telling children
"Don't be afraid, I'm your own dear Mother"
Expressing her desire to grant boons
To the devotees through the 'Varada Mudra'[4]!

---

[3] The Abhaya mudrā ("mudrā of no-fear") represents protection, peace, benevolence, and dispelling of fear.

[4] The Varada mudrā ("favourable mudrā") signifies offering, welcome, charity, giving, compassion and sincerity

The Divine Mother beheaded all evil forces
Of selfishness, jealousy, greed, lust, crime
Murdered in cold blood those who molested
Raped, oppressed, prostituted Mother Nature!

She is the Cosmic Womb giving birth
To all animate and inanimate living and nonliving!,
Shiva is the 'Ultimate Reality"
"The Brahman" the absolute
The Self, pure consciousness
Beyond all names, forms and activities!

Kali is his Shakti, expression of his
Bare absolute wild untamed ego
His dynamic active energy
Responsible for all names, forms and activities!

4

Ego exists but not without connected to Self
Kali cannot remain without attached to Shiva
She had to step on herself on Shiva's chest
She is the supreme consciousness of the world
The invisible, invincible supreme reality
She is the icon of extinction of evils
In the cosmos and in the microcosm, the mind!

Shakti and Shiva are united, non dualistic
Inseparably integrated like fire and power to burn
Joined in creative bliss, in divine copulation
Of active and static forces
Centripetal and centrifugal energy

Life and death are coexistent
Non dualistic death comes out of life
The Wheel of life turns bringing
Cycles of births and deaths!

5

After annihilation of the evil
Powerful negative forces of cosmos and microcosm
Kali prodded[5] her consort Shiva
To go ahead into the next cycle of creation
Like cultivating next cycle of crop
Bringing afresh a new world from the ashes
Both in the universe and in the microcosm of the mind
In the abyss, bottomless infinite Cosmic Womb
The light is born again in a Big Bang!

6

Being the mother of ten million million ...
Atomic and subatomic particles in the universe
The eternal supreme benevolent mother
Of energy appears, disappears out of nowhere
Spontaneously, giving birth to the energy
For dispersion ad infinitum producing limitless void
That has swallowed up everything
The black violent force of time and change
The state where time, space and causation
Have disappeared without any trace!

---

[5] *Nudged*

7

"Om Krim Kalyai Namah
Om Kapalinaye Namah
Om Hrim Shrim Krim Parameshvari
Kalike Svaha
Aum Sri Maha Kalikayai Namah!"

We bow to Goddess Kali,
The all powerful devastating time
The supreme energy of the world
We bow to the great divine Goddess Kali

We salute to the all powerful devastating
Divine Great Black Mother Goddess of Time!
We submit before the bottomless
'Cosmic Womb
That emptiness beyond emptiness'!
The infinite abyss uninterruptedly emptying
Itself in its fathomless dark void!

The celestial womb of time giving birth
To divine light in cycles of births and deaths
The Mother Nature, Prakriti, the 'womb
That gave birth to both the world and the God!'

Poem-52

COSMIC DANCE OF SHIVA

Yin and Yang have been omnipresent in the universe, explicit and implicit in varied forms in living and non living things. They are the energy vibes dependent on each other to become perfect and complete. Shakti and Shiva are other names of Yin and Yang and they have been appearing, disappearing and reappearing over the years in varied forms.

Yang narrates to Yin through this poem about the worst tragedy faced by Shiva and how he recovered from bitter realities of life. Yin and Yang know that they are united as one and the same, completing, complementing the supreme energy flow of the cosmos. Though nothing is complete without the two indispensable essential energy forms; they may exist dependent on each other like positive and negative electricity charges or polarities of the magnet.

Yang or Shiva is the King of all dances, known as Nataraja and believes in the two famous dance forms of Shiva, the cosmic dance of destruction known as Rudra Thandava and the cosmic dance of bliss or Aananda Thandava. Yang believes in the dance of bliss to live in happiness and adopts the formula to derive joy of living amidst life's compelling adverse circumstances.

Yang dances in the universe as well in the mind sky known as Chidambaram. This poem is about the King of all Dances, Shiva Nataraja. Yang believes in switching on the dance of bliss in the theatre of his mind. At times he has no escape but to perform the ultimate cosmic dance of destruction; especially when he is affected by negative vibes of the world.

1

Babe
Won't you like to hear
The tragic love story -
The legendary love
Of yogic lovers Shiva and Sati?

Daksha invited
All Gods and Goddesses for a Yagya
A religious sacrifice of great magnitude
The greatest Yagya
Ever performed in the universe
But not invited
His daughter Sati and son in law Shiva!

2

Depressed was Sati
But went to her father's sacrifice!
Uninvited was Sati
But went to Yagya
Ignoring Shiva's advice!

Embarrassed was Sati
But her father continued ridiculing
Dejected was Sati
But her father went on uttering ill of Shiva

Culminated
Agony, anger, sorrow
Pain, helplessness

Sati jumped into
The sacrificial fire
Self immolated!

3

Inconsolable
Uncontrollable
Raging with fury
Shiva wandered
Circumambulated the universe
Like a body severed into half
In severe intolerable morose
Carrying on his shoulder
His partner's burnt dead body!

Locks of matted hair
Thick like luxuriant Amazon rain forest
Spread all over
Stirring never-ending cyclones, tsunamis!

Ceaseless torrents
Cascading cataracts
Flood water of the Ganges
Caused holocaust, apocalypse
Unprecedented obliteration in the Milky Way!

Blazing inferno originated
From his third eye raged like wild fire
Blazed all over his forehead
Engulfing everything in the areole of fire!

Continued uninterruptedly
The cosmic dance
Outreaching limitless space
Crumbled down moon, stellar bodies
Shiva struck down everything in the universe!

4

DAMA....DUM... DUM...
DAMA...DUM...DAMA...DUM...DUM..
Reverberated sound of his drum
Fury turned into catastrophe!

Determined Vishnu
Followed Shiva with his 'Chakra' all over
Disposed off bit by bit
Sati's dead body, cutting with his Chakra
Endeavoured to end
Shiva's agony, sorrow, limitless fury and grief!

Fell all over the limbs
Of the corpse
Of the Mother Goddess
At 51 places
Fell in India, Nepal, Bangladesh
Tibet, Sri Lanka, Bhutan, Pakistan!

Fell 'Pada Khanda'
The lower part at Jagannath Puri in Orissa
Fell 'Stana Khanda'
The breast at Tara Tarini in Orissa

Fell 'Yoni Khanda'
The vulva at Kamakshi, Guwahati in Assam
Fell 'Mukha Khanda'
The face at Dakhina Kalika
In West Bengal and so on...

Fell her organs and ornaments
At hundred and eight places all over
Created 'Shakti Peethas'
The temples to worship the Mother Goddess!

5

Grief struck
Lost interest in life and duties
Shiva meditated in the Himalayan cave
Cosmic order went into a six!

In the absence of the Lord
Gods pleaded
To the Mother Goddess:
'Come, please; Goddess
Please do, come to earth
Come, please; in reincarnation
Please, do join your consort!'

Sati was reborn as Parvati
The benign Goddess
As daughter
Of the Mountain King of Himalayas!

Parvati did penance
Meditation, austerities
In intense longing
To be united with her consort!

Helpless was Parvati
In wooing her other half
Did she seek the help
Of the God and the Goddess of Love!

6

Blossomed spring
Transforming the cave
Into a sensuous
Pleasure Garden of Eden!
Filled with fragrant flowers, singing birds
Music of waterfalls, buzzing honey bees!

Kama, the God of Love
Lost no time to shoot yogi Shiva
With the arrows of desires one after another!

Distracted from meditation
Furious was the Lord
Opened his third eye
Incinerating Kama in blazing fire!

Parvati lost no time
Continued wooing her lover
Till united in Him
Bringing back order in the universe!

7

Let us offer prayers
To the great cosmic dancer
Lord Shiva 'Nataraja'!

The dancer who destroys
Bad and evil in the microcosm
And macrocosm
The dancer who induces
Ecstasy, divinity, spirituality
Eliminating evil thoughts!

The dancer who unites
Earth, water, fire, air
Ether, mind, intellect, ego!

The dancer who annihilates
Everything in the cosmos
To sow seeds of new lives!

The dancer who cleanses of evils
From the microcosm
To sow seeds of new thoughts!

The dancer who rotates
The wheel of life
Bringing creation after destruction!

The dancer who brings
Cycles of destruction, creation
Deaths, births in the cosmos!

Like a farmer who sows afresh
Ploughing his land
After harvesting the earlier crops!

8

Let us prostrate before the Lord
Surrendering our ego
Subjugating our arrogance
Subduing our 'I' consciousness!

In absolute humility
Spellbound in His splendour
In His rhythm, beauty
Vibrancy, power and grace
At the feet of Shiva Nataraja[1]
Of **Chidambaram:**
In the sky of the mind!

Oh! Lord
You are incarnated here
In absolute formlessness
In Lingam formed
Of ether, space, air, sky!

9

Let us pay homage to you
Bless us Lord

---

[1] The dancing Shiva, the God of destruction in Hindu mythology at Chidambaram temple located in Tamil Nadu, India. Chidambaram means the sky of consciousness. Shiva dances at Chidambaram, in the cosmos and in the sky of consciousness after annihilation of ego.

We bowed to you
In all your five forms:
All your five Shiva Lingams[2]
Made of earth, fire, water, air and ether!
Oh! Lord!
You are the king of the ultimate dance
The dancer who dissolves into his dance
In the **dance of bliss - Aananda Thandava**
In the dance of destruction - Rudra Thandava
In '[3]the dance of subatomic particles'!

10

You're the father of all dances
The Cosmic dancer Shiva:
The dancer who holds the secret
Knowledge of creation, protection and destruction!
The dancer who dances
In the consciousness
The creator, the preserver and the destroyer!

All in one or one in three aspects as you incarnate
The maker of the Milky Way, galaxies, stellar bodies
Existing all through the cycles of births and deaths
Of the living, animate inanimate, human beings!

11

Master! You present as a pillar of fire
Originating from the abyss of the universe

---

[2] A stone pillar having an iconic and phallic connotation in Hindu Mythology used for worship of Shiva.
[3] Fritjof Capra says in his book "The Tao of Physics" (1976)

Extending beyond the heaven above!
Lord let you dance in our 'Chidambaram'
In the sanctum sanctorum of the temple of our mind!

Let you enter
Into our inner consciousness
At **Chidambaram -**
In the limitless cosmos of the mind
Let our ego be annihilated
Let the dance of bliss continue
Let the cosmic dance of bliss
Continue uninterrupted in our mind!

12

You are the supreme consciousness
Of the universe
Let the cosmic cycles
Of creation, protection, destruction go on!

"Aum Namah Shivaya!"
"Aum Namo Bhagavate Rudraya Namah!"

"Sarve Bhavantu Sukhinah
Sarve Santu Niramayah
Sarve Bhadrani Pasyantu
Ma Kaschit Dukha Bhagbhavet!"

Om! May all be happy
May all be healthy!
May we all experience what is good!
Let no one suffer!

13

We felt our mind diving deep
Into the ocean of consciousness
We realized our body trembling
In trance in the cosmic rays
We experienced the cosmic rays raining
Pouring down from the space beyond!

In the cascading energy flow
The earth, air, rocks, sand, sea
Flora, fauna, animate, inanimate
Molecules, atoms, particles danced
Continued vibrating, colliding,
Interacting, communicating, intermixing
Attacking, destroying one another!
In the cosmic dance of the energy
We felt the rhythm of His steps!

14

We heard
The song, music, sound of drums
We realized
We were part of the cosmic dance
Of the King of all dancers - Shiva Nataraja!

Call it Particle Physics
Quantum mechanics
Atomic physics
The theory of relativity
'The Tao of Physics'!

Let us merge into the energy
Of the supreme consciousness
Let us unite as one in the
Supreme divine energy flow!
Like Shiva Parvati united
In Ardhanareeshwara
The two energy forms
Merging into one body!

Poem-53

SHRI CHAKRA
GEOMETRY OF THE SEED OF CREATION

Yin & Yang are integral part of the Cosmic Womb. The couple is amazed by the ingenuity of the human being in capturing their romance, union and interaction in Tantric symbolism and imagery.

They are particularly impressed by Shri Chakra! Being inseparably united they meet and mate, unite and disunite as light and its radiation, fire and heat, static and dynamic dimensions of energy flow, negative and positive current flow of the electricity, south and north polarity of the earth and magnetism.

As has been his wont throughout ages since the very beginning even before the Big Bang hypothesis of the origin of universe, Yang wants to share his ideas of Shri Yantra with Yin. He shares the secret of the mathematics and geometry of creation with his love Yin. He tells Yin that Shri Chakra or Shri Yantra is the ultimate mathematical representation of the mystery of creation and the origin of life in the universe like the Einstein's energy equation.

I

Do you remember, Babe
That day
When we were
Before the sanctum sanctorum
At Mookambika temple in Karnataka!

Adi Shankaracharya installed
The Shri Chakra of Shri Devi
Before the unique
'Ardhanareeshvara lingam'?

You showed me
The lingam
Split into two halves
The female left half Shakti stands taller
Than the male right half Shiva, her consort!

Your eyes were gleaming
In the golden halo
In the sun rays
Reflected from the top of the lingam!

You told smiling in pride:
"Darling
See, greater is the power
Of our goddess!

Tell me, now
Who rotates
This Wheel of Life:
The wheel that cycles ceaselessly
Creating, preserving, destroying
The cosmos and the microcosm
The universe, the living
Human being
And the microcosm?"

2

Exhilarated were we
In the energy vibes of
Shri Chakra!

The geometry of the mystic cosmic womb
Of creation, destruction and preservation
Of microcosm and the macrocosm!
Exhibiting the Yin and Yang of energy
Engaged in the mystery matrix of creation!
The geometry of the mystery
Of the living and the universe!

The imagery
Of the divine energy
The spiritual equation
Of the supreme power
Like Einstein's equation
On matter and energy!

3

You loved not geometry at school
But you loved the geometry of creation!
Drawn with mathematical precision
The interpenetrating nine triangles!
Give birth to
Forty three triangles!

Encircled by two lotuses:
Eight and sixteen petalled

Encompassed by three circles:
Contained in a rectangular enclosure
With four sides and four doors
Like the temple of the mind!

    4

"Darling, tell me; please
What do these triangles for?"

"**Shakti** is represented by
The five female triangles
With apex downwards!
See the Shakti triangles
Meets and mates **Shiva**
The four male triangles
With apex upwards!

These triangles are
The metaphor for the
Microcosm
And the cosmos!

The merging of
The 'I' consciousness and
The supreme consciousness!
The rising apex of the triangles
Symbolizes the urge of the soul
To rise to the Supreme Being!
The apex of the inverted triangles
Reciprocate, intermingle, and merge!"

5

"Let us pray
To the **Goddess Tripura Sundhari**
Three goddesses united in one
Shakti, Lakshmi, Saraswati
Goddess of power, wealth, knowledge
The ruling deity of Shri Chakra

Isn't she manifested
Splendidly in three forms
The young
The beautiful
And the terrific!

The triangle represents
The three worlds
The three dimensions of nature
The three cosmic activities
Of creation, maintenance and destruction
Brahma, Vishnu and Shiva
The states of past, present and future!

6

The triangles manifest
The three gunas
'Satva', 'Rajas' and 'Tamas'!
The symbol of Sun
The Moon and Fire!
The will, knowledge and action!

The three stages
Of sleep
Dream and waking up
While we are awake
We are partly asleep
While we are asleep
We are partly in dreams!"

7

Delighted were we
In the brilliance
Witnessing the lotus petals
Blossoming in bliss
In the luminosity of wisdom
In the sunlight of true knowledge!

Spellbound were we
Being attracted towards
The irrepressible energy pool from the centre
Radiating from the central point-**Bindu**
Of the red inverted triangle of creation!

8

You read out to me; enlightened
"See Darling
Lalita the goddess is red
Like the light of thousand rising suns
Attired in red
She symbolizies 'Rajo guna'
The colour of desire, passion, activity!

See Shiva is white in colour
Radiating light
Reflection of the light
Is his consort Shakti!
The colour of dawn
The harbinger of light!"

9

We witnessed the feminine energy
Engulfing the masculine
The red Shakti point merged
Into the white Shiva point
Shiva and **Shakti**
United to form **Shivalinga**
The symbol of Ardhanareeshvara:
In the female-the epicenter of life
In it entered the line symbolizing the male!

The seed of the creation is impregnated
In the inverted base triangle of Shri Chakra
In the central red point 'Bindu' chakra
The forty fourth point triangle in Shri Chakra!

10

We were mystified
By the symbol of the limitless
Amazed perceiving the imperceptible
Astounded locating the seed of consciousness
Impregnated where Shiva Shakti united!

Shiva Bindu
The point denoting static energy
Merged with shakti Bindu
The point denoting dynamic energy
The three Bindus united in the primary triangle
The triangle
That indicates the origin of universe!

The primary triangle evolved
Into other geometric forms
Square, pentagon, hexagon
Octagon, polygon and so on
Circles and innumerable
Polymorphic contours
Symbolizing creation
Of the Supreme Being
The primordial Mother Goddess!

11

'Nada'
The sound of the origin of the universe
The sound of the drum
Damru' of Shiva
Interspersed in between the
'Lalita Sahasranam' –
Thousand names of the goddess!

Multitude of unending universes
Presided over by their own trinities
Of Brahmas, Vishnus, and Shivas
With their spouses

Sarasvatis Lakshmis and Gaouris
Tripura Sundhari
The ruling Supreme Power
Of the Multiple Universes!

12

Infatuated by the intensity
Of the illumination
We prostrated in reverence
Before **Shridevi** in **Shri Chakra!**

In front of the imagery
Of the mount of creation
Meditation started
From the outer chakra
Moving towards the inner core
Reaching the very soul!

The state where "I and you'
'Exist and not exist'
The state where nothing is clear
'To be done' or 'not to be done'!

13

The Pujari explained:
"In the womb of creation
Of the cosmos and the microcosm
In the inner triangle
The Venus Love Pyramid of creation!
At the central point red 'Bindu'

Tripura Sundhari is born in lotus:
Like a flower is born in a flower!

The two lilies are born
In the lotus
Two lovely lilies
Like eyes on lotus like face!
Of 'Atirahasya Yogini'
The secret goddess of yogic powers!

14

The 'Sarvanandamaya' is replete with bliss
In which the 'Lalita Maha Tripura Sundhari'
Is adored, worshipped in her supreme glory
With flowers; kumkum[1]; and mantra chanting!"

Ecstatic by the obscurity of the creation
I saluted **Maha Tripura Sundhari:**
Oh! Mother of all mothers
The Divine mother of the Cosmos
Oh! **Mahamaya** I bow to thee
You revolve The Wheel of Life!

Jai Ho! Mookambika!
Tripura Sundhari! Kamalambika!
Mother of all universes
Rejoicing and resting
On the lap of the almighty

---

[1] powder used for social and religious markings in Hinduism

Shivakamashwara
The God who fulfills all desires!

15

We performed **Puja**
Before the Sanctum Sanctorum

Offering **Niranjana** to the Sun
The light waving ceremony
Returning the Sun its light!

We offered **Arrghya** to the Moon
The water that is due to it!

We offered **Tarpana** to the ocean
Returning what belongs to it!

"Om Bhur Bhuvahsvaha
Tat Savitur Varenyam
Bargo Devasya Dheemahi
Diyo Yo Nah Prachodayaat!"

16

We meditated
On the supreme divine reality
The source of the three worlds
The embodiment of knowledge and light!
Destroyer of all sins and ignorance
May the Almighty stimulate our intelligence
May we realize the ultimate truth!

17

Babe
Let us continue our meditation!
Let the divine energy flow
Let it merge, and unite
Let it encircle us
Let it envelope us
Let it spread around, disseminate!

Let us perform
'Nava Avarana Puja'
All that take us to bliss!
Let us accept
The symbolic
Cloak that obscures
Let us admit
The vision of the ultimate truth!

18

Let us admit
The negative forces that obstruct
Let us be not disillusioned
Let us see
The ultimate truth 'Brahman'!

Let us meditate listening
To the inner sound of life!
Let us listen to the inner voice
The whisper of our mind!

Let us listen to the sound
From the cavern of the heart
'Nada'!
The sound that brought us
In this world!

19

Let us chant Mantras
Let the air be reverberated by prayers
Let the vibration spread around
And overwhelm the being!

Let us delve deep
Into the ocean of the mind
Let us delve deep into
Feelings, emotions and thoughts

Let us experience
The divine energy flow within us
Let the divine light of the Shri Chakra
Enter into the consciousness!

20

Let the divine light merge
Into the supreme energy flow of the universe
Let us be blessed by the supreme Bliss
Of Self Discovery and Self Realization
Let us be blessed by the deity ruling
The sanctum sanctorum of our mind!

Let us open our inner eye
Realize the ultimate truth
'Sat Chit Ananda',
Let us be enlightened by the luminosity
Of Self Realization, Self Actualization!

21

Babe, let us intensify our meditation
Unlocking the doors of the mind
Let us unravel, open
And realize the mysteries
Of the mind by the key of meditation!

22

Puja continued
Pujari explained:
"Now you can meditate on Aum
Aum Brahman is the ultimate reality
Aum is the "Pranava Mantra"
The source of all Mantras
The primordial vibration is Aum
Beyond existence, before existence!
Creation consists of vibrations 'shabda'
The continuous chanting of mantra
Purifies mind and consciousness
Thoughts and feelings are soundless vibrations!"

23

Babe, now we know
The game of Yin & Yang

Is the game of night and day
The game of darkness and light
The game of envy and love!

The day breaks out
From the womb of darkness
The darkness leads
To breaking of daylight!

Happiness is the seed
Deeply concealed in sorrow
Sorrow gradually grows
Into the tree of happiness!

Success is the seed
Impregnated in the womb of failure
Failure gives birth to success
After the gestation period and labour pains!

24

I am aware
I am not me alone
As I exist not without me
You are the very extension of me
You are me reflected to make the whole

You and I are the two sides of being
The two forms of the same existence
What makes you happy is my happiness
What makes you sexy is my sexiness!

Pujari narrated Shankaracharya's
"Soundarya Lahiri"
"The waves of happiness and waves of beauty"
Citing the 'Pancha Dasakshari Mantra'
The twenty five seed letter Mantra
Worshipping Tripura Sundhari,
The ruling deity in the Shri Chakra!:

"She who is the mother of us all
The seed letter ka of my lord Shiva
The seed letter a of goddess Shakti
The seed letter ee of god of love,
The seed letter la of earth,
The seed letter ha of the sun god,
The seed letter sa of the moon with cool rays,
The seed letter ka of again the god of love,
The seed letter ha of the sky,
The seed letter ha of Indra, the king of devas or gods,
The seed letter sa of Para,
The seed letter ka of the god of love,
The seed letter la of the Lord Vishnu,
Along with your seed letter Hrim,
Which joins at the end of each of the three holy wheels,
Became the holy word to worship you"

25
"Om Aim Hreem Shreem
Shri Lalita Tripurasundari
Padukam Poojayami Namah"

" Ka E I La Hreem —
Ha Sa Ka Ha La Hreem -
Sa Ka La Hreem"

"Panchami pancha bhooteshi
Pancha sankhyopacharini"

Poem-54

THE BLISS

Yin and Yang understand the meaning of life from the primordial days of the Cosmic Womb. They know human life is precious and each moment can make a difference not only in one's life, but also in the lives of others around and the world in which one lives. What they believe in is to fill in the love hungry world with positive energy vibes of kindness, compassion and concern; because, they believe that the human clock or the time machine put in the heart by the creator or the maker can stop any time; because the time for enacting the role in the drama or performance called life will be over at any moment. It can be so smooth sometime that the role in the unreal world can be time barred even without one realising it. This can happen unconsciously over a dream for the lucky chosen ones instead of being a vegetable like existence in ICU or in a ventilator decomposing the parts gradually. When time is out, the time machine of the Almighty can be put off from further ticking even in the case of the so called powerful All Mighty by the Almighty!

Yang feels that when life is lived full, enjoyed full, there should be complete contentment when one finally says goodbye from the scene of this unreal world after completing his assigned role in the drama called life or play or game of life with its own rules. The river of life may meander hither thither along the risky dangerous rocky terrains. The journey of life can be a roller coaster pleasure ride provided one feels content and understands the very purpose of life, witnesses and oversees everything just as an onlooker without being in an illusion of having been entrapped into the narrow bottled precious jar in the famous well known fable of the Zen Master!

I

Empowered, if I were
My Creator
I would metamorphose into wind
Spreading fragrance of love!

Empowered, if I were
My Maker
I would transform into inferno
Engulfing all the evils in the world!

Empowered, if I were
My Lord
I would convert myself
Into an Ocean
Absorbing sublime
Love in the universe!

Empowered, if I were
My God!
I would merge into the Sun
Charioting the seven horses
Forming the seven colours of light
Chasing darkness in the horizon
Around the globe, around the cosmos
Around the Milky Way endlessly ad infinitum
Catching up, wooing, hugging darkness

Embracing and merging into darkness
Enveloping night into day!

I know still in the womb of light
Seed of darkness will grow
Big and bigger dwindling the illumination
Swallowing light completely by the darkness
Chasing day light by darkness
And eating up day by night!

2

Oh! My Master!
You made me aware
This voyage
Called life
Began with no role of mine!
You chose the actors
You determined the time and place
You made it happen
In the first do or die race of life!

Oh! My Guru!
Let the Storm in me be calm
Let the Fire in me be put off
Let the Ocean in me be quiet
Let the Earth in me merge into dust
Let the Ether in me settle
In the space above!

3

I am aware
I came from the real world
Into this unreal world
Made of illusion
As a guest for a while
Just to play the drama called life!

I love to live in each moment
I enjoy each moment of the act
Of this drama called life!
No regrets!
No pain!
No illusions, any more!

4

I know the credits and debits
Will be adjusted!
The profit and loss account
Of life will be finalised!
The Balance Sheet of life
Will be drawn and finally certified
Before this unreal journey of life
Is over in the unreal world
Before merging into
The supreme eternal energy flow!

5

I am aware
The Air in me

The Water in me
The Earth in me
The Fire in me
The Ether in me:
Will settle down
Only and only
When I disintegrate
Into the basic
Elements of life:
Only when
I dissolve this container
This garment
Into its constituents
And me ultimately
Merging into Thee!